I0351243

C-2313 CAREER EXAMINATION SERIES

This is your PASSBOOK for...

Tax Auditor

Test Preparation Study Guide
Questions & Answers

NLC®
NATIONAL LEARNING CORPORATION®

National Learning Corporation

212 Michael Drive, Syosset, NY 11791
(516) 921-8888 • www.passbooks.com
E-mail: info@passbooks.com

PASSBOOK® SERIES

THE *PASSBOOK® SERIES* has been created to prepare applicants and candidates for the ultimate academic battlefield – the examination room.

At some time in our lives, each and every one of us may be required to take an examination – for validation, matriculation, admission, qualification, registration, certification, or licensure.

Based on the assumption that every applicant or candidate has met the basic formal educational standards, has taken the required number of courses, and read the necessary texts, the *PASSBOOK® SERIES* furnishes the one special preparation which may assure passing with confidence, instead of failing with insecurity. Examination questions – together with answers – are furnished as the basic vehicle for study so that the mysteries of the examination and its compounding difficulties may be eliminated or diminished by a sure method.

This book is meant to help you pass your examination provided that you qualify and are serious in your objective.

The entire field is reviewed through the huge store of content information which is succinctly presented through a provocative and challenging approach – the question-and-answer method.

A climate of success is established by furnishing the correct answers at the end of each test.

You soon learn to recognize types of questions, forms of questions, and patterns of questioning. You may even begin to anticipate expected outcomes.

You perceive that many questions are repeated or adapted so that you can gain acute insights, which may enable you to score many sure points.

You learn how to confront new questions, or types of questions, and to attack them confidently and work out the correct answers.

You note objectives and emphases, and recognize pitfalls and dangers, so that you may make positive educational adjustments.

Moreover, you are kept fully informed in relation to new concepts, methods, practices, and directions in the field.

You discover that you are actually taking the examination all the time: you are preparing for the examination by "taking" an examination, not by reading extraneous and/or supererogatory textbooks.

In short, this PASSBOOK®, used directedly, should be an important factor in helping you to pass your test.

TAX AUDITOR

DUTIES

A Tax Auditor, under general direction, heads a squad engaged in complex field audits of books and records of taxpayers. A Tax Auditor develops overall audit plans and assumes responsibility for their execution and arranges for working papers to be prepared in conformity with professional standards and for documentary support of the audit. Field audits may be conducted in or out of the state, and Tax Auditors will be required to spend considerable time in the field.

SUBJECT OF EXAMINATION

The multiple-choice test may include questions on generally accepted accounting principles and auditing standards; Federal taxation; communication skills and English usage; reading comprehension; arithmetic computation; and related areas.

HOW TO TAKE A TEST

I. YOU MUST PASS AN EXAMINATION

A. WHAT EVERY CANDIDATE SHOULD KNOW

Examination applicants often ask us for help in preparing for the written test. What can I study in advance? What kinds of questions will be asked? How will the test be given? How will the papers be graded?

As an applicant for a civil service examination, you may be wondering about some of these things. Our purpose here is to suggest effective methods of advance study and to describe civil service examinations.

Your chances for success on this examination can be increased if you know how to prepare. Those "pre-examination jitters" can be reduced if you know what to expect. You can even experience an adventure in good citizenship if you know why civil service exams are given.

B. WHY ARE CIVIL SERVICE EXAMINATIONS GIVEN?

Civil service examinations are important to you in two ways. As a citizen, you want public jobs filled by employees who know how to do their work. As a job seeker, you want a fair chance to compete for that job on an equal footing with other candidates. The best-known means of accomplishing this two-fold goal is the competitive examination.

Exams are widely publicized throughout the nation. They may be administered for jobs in federal, state, city, municipal, town or village governments or agencies.

Any citizen may apply, with some limitations, such as the age or residence of applicants. Your experience and education may be reviewed to see whether you meet the requirements for the particular examination. When these requirements exist, they are reasonable and applied consistently to all applicants. Thus, a competitive examination may cause you some uneasiness now, but it is your privilege and safeguard.

C. HOW ARE CIVIL SERVICE EXAMS DEVELOPED?

Examinations are carefully written by trained technicians who are specialists in the field known as "psychological measurement," in consultation with recognized authorities in the field of work that the test will cover. These experts recommend the subject matter areas or skills to be tested; only those knowledges or skills important to your success on the job are included. The most reliable books and source materials available are used as references. Together, the experts and technicians judge the difficulty level of the questions.

Test technicians know how to phrase questions so that the problem is clearly stated. Their ethics do not permit "trick" or "catch" questions. Questions may have been tried out on sample groups, or subjected to statistical analysis, to determine their usefulness.

Written tests are often used in combination with performance tests, ratings of training and experience, and oral interviews. All of these measures combine to form the best-known means of finding the right person for the right job.

II. HOW TO PASS THE WRITTEN TEST

A. NATURE OF THE EXAMINATION

To prepare intelligently for civil service examinations, you should know how they differ from school examinations you have taken. In school you were assigned certain definite pages to read or subjects to cover. The examination questions were quite detailed and usually emphasized memory. Civil service exams, on the other hand, try to discover your present ability to perform the duties of a position, plus your potentiality to learn these duties. In other words, a civil service exam attempts to predict how successful you will be. Questions cover such a broad area that they cannot be as minute and detailed as school exam questions.

In the public service similar kinds of work, or positions, are grouped together in one "class." This process is known as *position-classification.* All the positions in a class are paid according to the salary range for that class. One class title covers all of these positions, and they are all tested by the same examination.

B. FOUR BASIC STEPS

1) Study the announcement

How, then, can you know what subjects to study? Our best answer is: "Learn as much as possible about the class of positions for which you've applied." The exam will test the knowledge, skills and abilities needed to do the work.

Your most valuable source of information about the position you want is the official exam announcement. This announcement lists the training and experience qualifications. Check these standards and apply only if you come reasonably close to meeting them.

The brief description of the position in the examination announcement offers some clues to the subjects which will be tested. Think about the job itself. Review the duties in your mind. Can you perform them, or are there some in which you are rusty? Fill in the blank spots in your preparation.

Many jurisdictions preview the written test in the exam announcement by including a section called "Knowledge and Abilities Required," "Scope of the Examination," or some similar heading. Here you will find out specifically what fields will be tested.

2) Review your own background

Once you learn in general what the position is all about, and what you need to know to do the work, ask yourself which subjects you already know fairly well and which need improvement. You may wonder whether to concentrate on improving your strong areas or on building some background in your fields of weakness. When the announcement has specified "some knowledge" or "considerable knowledge," or has used adjectives like "beginning principles of..." or "advanced ... methods," you can get a clue as to the number and difficulty of questions to be asked in any given field. More questions, and hence broader coverage, would be included for those subjects which are more important in the work. Now weigh your strengths and weaknesses against the job requirements and prepare accordingly.

3) Determine the level of the position

Another way to tell how intensively you should prepare is to understand the level of the job for which you are applying. Is it the entering level? In other words, is this the position in which beginners in a field of work are hired? Or is it an intermediate or advanced level? Sometimes this is indicated by such words as "Junior" or "Senior" in the class title. Other jurisdictions use Roman numerals to designate the level – Clerk I, Clerk II, for example. The word "Supervisor" sometimes appears in the title. If the level is not indicated by the title, check the description of duties. Will you be working under very close supervision, or will you have responsibility for independent decisions in this work?

4) Choose appropriate study materials

Now that you know the subjects to be examined and the relative amount of each subject to be covered, you can choose suitable study materials. For beginning level jobs, or even advanced ones, if you have a pronounced weakness in some aspect of your training, read a modern, standard textbook in that field. Be sure it is up to date and has general coverage. Such books are normally available at your library, and the librarian will be glad to help you locate one. For entry-level positions, questions of appropriate difficulty are chosen – neither highly advanced questions, nor those too simple. Such questions require careful thought but not advanced training.

If the position for which you are applying is technical or advanced, you will read more advanced, specialized material. If you are already familiar with the basic principles of your field, elementary textbooks would waste your time. Concentrate on advanced textbooks and technical periodicals. Think through the concepts and review difficult problems in your field.

These are all general sources. You can get more ideas on your own initiative, following these leads. For example, training manuals and publications of the government agency which employs workers in your field can be useful, particularly for technical and professional positions. A letter or visit to the government department involved may result in more specific study suggestions, and certainly will provide you with a more definite idea of the exact nature of the position you are seeking.

III. KINDS OF TESTS

Tests are used for purposes other than measuring knowledge and ability to perform specified duties. For some positions, it is equally important to test ability to make adjustments to new situations or to profit from training. In others, basic mental abilities not dependent on information are essential. Questions which test these things may not appear as pertinent to the duties of the position as those which test for knowledge and information. Yet they are often highly important parts of a fair examination. For very general questions, it is almost impossible to help you direct your study efforts. What we can do is to point out some of the more common of these general abilities needed in public service positions and describe some typical questions.

1) General information

Broad, general information has been found useful for predicting job success in some kinds of work. This is tested in a variety of ways, from vocabulary lists to questions about current events. Basic background in some field of work, such as sociology or economics, may be sampled in a group of questions. Often these are principles which have become familiar to most persons through exposure rather than through formal training. It is difficult to advise you how to study for these questions; being alert to the world around you is our best suggestion.

2) Verbal ability

An example of an ability needed in many positions is verbal or language ability. Verbal ability is, in brief, the ability to use and understand words. Vocabulary and grammar tests are typical measures of this ability. Reading comprehension or paragraph interpretation questions are common in many kinds of civil service tests. You are given a paragraph of written material and asked to find its central meaning.

3) Numerical ability

Number skills can be tested by the familiar arithmetic problem, by checking paired lists of numbers to see which are alike and which are different, or by interpreting charts and graphs. In the latter test, a graph may be printed in the test booklet which you are asked to use as the basis for answering questions.

4) Observation

A popular test for law-enforcement positions is the observation test. A picture is shown to you for several minutes, then taken away. Questions about the picture test your ability to observe both details and larger elements.

5) Following directions

In many positions in the public service, the employee must be able to carry out written instructions dependably and accurately. You may be given a chart with several columns, each column listing a variety of information. The questions require you to carry out directions involving the information given in the chart.

6) Skills and aptitudes

Performance tests effectively measure some manual skills and aptitudes. When the skill is one in which you are trained, such as typing or shorthand, you can practice. These tests are often very much like those given in business school or high school courses. For many of the other skills and aptitudes, however, no short-time preparation can be made. Skills and abilities natural to you or that you have developed throughout your lifetime are being tested.

Many of the general questions just described provide all the data needed to answer the questions and ask you to use your reasoning ability to find the answers. Your best preparation for these tests, as well as for tests of facts and ideas, is to be at your physical and mental best. You, no doubt, have your own methods of getting into an exam-taking mood and keeping "in shape." The next section lists some ideas on this subject.

IV. KINDS OF QUESTIONS

Only rarely is the "essay" question, which you answer in narrative form, used in civil service tests. Civil service tests are usually of the short-answer type. Full instructions for answering these questions will be given to you at the examination. But in case this is your first experience with short-answer questions and separate answer sheets, here is what you need to know:

1) Multiple-choice Questions

Most popular of the short-answer questions is the "multiple choice" or "best answer" question. It can be used, for example, to test for factual knowledge, ability to solve problems or judgment in meeting situations found at work.

A multiple-choice question is normally one of three types—

- It can begin with an incomplete statement followed by several possible endings. You are to find the one ending which *best* completes the statement, although some of the others may not be entirely wrong.
- It can also be a complete statement in the form of a question which is answered by choosing one of the statements listed.

- It can be in the form of a problem – again you select the best answer.

Here is an example of a multiple-choice question with a discussion which should give you some clues as to the method for choosing the right answer:

When an employee has a complaint about his assignment, the action which will *best* help him overcome his difficulty is to
A. discuss his difficulty with his coworkers
B. take the problem to the head of the organization
C. take the problem to the person who gave him the assignment
D. say nothing to anyone about his complaint

In answering this question, you should study each of the choices to find which is best. Consider choice "A" – Certainly an employee may discuss his complaint with fellow employees, but no change or improvement can result, and the complaint remains unresolved. Choice "B" is a poor choice since the head of the organization probably does not know what assignment you have been given, and taking your problem to him is known as "going over the head" of the supervisor. The supervisor, or person who made the assignment, is the person who can clarify it or correct any injustice. Choice "C" is, therefore, correct. To say nothing, as in choice "D," is unwise. Supervisors have and interest in knowing the problems employees are facing, and the employee is seeking a solution to his problem.

2) True/False Questions

The "true/false" or "right/wrong" form of question is sometimes used. Here a complete statement is given. Your job is to decide whether the statement is right or wrong.

SAMPLE: A roaming cell-phone call to a nearby city costs less than a non-roaming call to a distant city.

This statement is wrong, or false, since roaming calls are more expensive.

This is not a complete list of all possible question forms, although most of the others are variations of these common types. You will always get complete directions for answering questions. Be sure you understand *how* to mark your answers – ask questions until you do.

V. RECORDING YOUR ANSWERS

Computer terminals are used more and more today for many different kinds of exams.

For an examination with very few applicants, you may be told to record your answers in the test booklet itself. Separate answer sheets are much more common. If this separate answer sheet is to be scored by machine – and this is often the case – it is highly important that you mark your answers correctly in order to get credit.

An electronic scoring machine is often used in civil service offices because of the speed with which papers can be scored. Machine-scored answer sheets must be marked with a pencil, which will be given to you. This pencil has a high graphite content which responds to the electronic scoring machine. As a matter of fact, stray dots may register as answers, so do not let your pencil rest on the answer sheet while you are pondering the correct answer. Also, if your pencil lead breaks or is otherwise defective, ask for another.

Since the answer sheet will be dropped in a slot in the scoring machine, be careful not to bend the corners or get the paper crumpled.

The answer sheet normally has five vertical columns of numbers, with 30 numbers to a column. These numbers correspond to the question numbers in your test booklet. After each number, going across the page are four or five pairs of dotted lines. These short dotted lines have small letters or numbers above them. The first two pairs may also have a "T" or "F" above the letters. This indicates that the first two pairs only are to be used if the questions are of the true-false type. If the questions are multiple choice, disregard the "T" and "F" and pay attention only to the small letters or numbers.

Answer your questions in the manner of the sample that follows:

32. The largest city in the United States is
    - A. Washington, D.C.
    - B. New York City
    - C. Chicago
    - D. Detroit
    - E. San Francisco

1) Choose the answer you think is best. (New York City is the largest, so "B" is correct.)
2) Find the row of dotted lines numbered the same as the question you are answering. (Find row number 32)
3) Find the pair of dotted lines corresponding to the answer. (Find the pair of lines under the mark "B.")
4) Make a solid black mark between the dotted lines.

VI. BEFORE THE TEST

Common sense will help you find procedures to follow to get ready for an examination. Too many of us, however, overlook these sensible measures. Indeed, nervousness and fatigue have been found to be the most serious reasons why applicants fail to do their best on civil service tests. Here is a list of reminders:

- Begin your preparation early – Don't wait until the last minute to go scurrying around for books and materials or to find out what the position is all about.
- Prepare continuously – An hour a night for a week is better than an all-night cram session. This has been definitely established. What is more, a night a week for a month will return better dividends than crowding your study into a shorter period of time.
- Locate the place of the exam – You have been sent a notice telling you when and where to report for the examination. If the location is in a different town or otherwise unfamiliar to you, it would be well to inquire the best route and learn something about the building.
- Relax the night before the test – Allow your mind to rest. Do not study at all that night. Plan some mild recreation or diversion; then go to bed early and get a good night's sleep.
- Get up early enough to make a leisurely trip to the place for the test – This way unforeseen events, traffic snarls, unfamiliar buildings, etc. will not upset you.
- Dress comfortably – A written test is not a fashion show. You will be known by number and not by name, so wear something comfortable.

- Leave excess paraphernalia at home – Shopping bags and odd bundles will get in your way. You need bring only the items mentioned in the official notice you received; usually everything you need is provided. Do not bring reference books to the exam. They will only confuse those last minutes and be taken away from you when in the test room.
- Arrive somewhat ahead of time – If because of transportation schedules you must get there very early, bring a newspaper or magazine to take your mind off yourself while waiting.
- Locate the examination room – When you have found the proper room, you will be directed to the seat or part of the room where you will sit. Sometimes you are given a sheet of instructions to read while you are waiting. Do not fill out any forms until you are told to do so; just read them and be prepared.
- Relax and prepare to listen to the instructions
- If you have any physical problem that may keep you from doing your best, be sure to tell the test administrator. If you are sick or in poor health, you really cannot do your best on the exam. You can come back and take the test some other time.

VII. AT THE TEST

The day of the test is here and you have the test booklet in your hand. The temptation to get going is very strong. Caution! There is more to success than knowing the right answers. You must know how to identify your papers and understand variations in the type of short-answer question used in this particular examination. Follow these suggestions for maximum results from your efforts:

1) Cooperate with the monitor

The test administrator has a duty to create a situation in which you can be as much at ease as possible. He will give instructions, tell you when to begin, check to see that you are marking your answer sheet correctly, and so on. He is not there to guard you, although he will see that your competitors do not take unfair advantage. He wants to help you do your best.

2) Listen to all instructions

Don't jump the gun! Wait until you understand all directions. In most civil service tests you get more time than you need to answer the questions. So don't be in a hurry. Read each word of instructions until you clearly understand the meaning. Study the examples, listen to all announcements and follow directions. Ask questions if you do not understand what to do.

3) Identify your papers

Civil service exams are usually identified by number only. You will be assigned a number; you must not put your name on your test papers. Be sure to copy your number correctly. Since more than one exam may be given, copy your exact examination title.

4) Plan your time

Unless you are told that a test is a "speed" or "rate of work" test, speed itself is usually not important. Time enough to answer all the questions will be provided, but this does not mean that you have all day. An overall time limit has been set. Divide the total time (in minutes) by the number of questions to determine the approximate time you have for each question.

5) Do not linger over difficult questions

If you come across a difficult question, mark it with a paper clip (useful to have along) and come back to it when you have been through the booklet. One caution if you do this – be sure to skip a number on your answer sheet as well. Check often to be sure that you have not lost your place and that you are marking in the row numbered the same as the question you are answering.

6) Read the questions

Be sure you know what the question asks! Many capable people are unsuccessful because they failed to *read* the questions correctly.

7) Answer all questions

Unless you have been instructed that a penalty will be deducted for incorrect answers, it is better to guess than to omit a question.

8) Speed tests

It is often better NOT to guess on speed tests. It has been found that on timed tests people are tempted to spend the last few seconds before time is called in marking answers at random – without even reading them – in the hope of picking up a few extra points. To discourage this practice, the instructions may warn you that your score will be "corrected" for guessing. That is, a penalty will be applied. The incorrect answers will be deducted from the correct ones, or some other penalty formula will be used.

9) Review your answers

If you finish before time is called, go back to the questions you guessed or omitted to give them further thought. Review other answers if you have time.

10) Return your test materials

If you are ready to leave before others have finished or time is called, take ALL your materials to the monitor and leave quietly. Never take any test material with you. The monitor can discover whose papers are not complete, and taking a test booklet may be grounds for disqualification.

VIII. EXAMINATION TECHNIQUES

1) Read the general instructions carefully. These are usually printed on the first page of the exam booklet. As a rule, these instructions refer to the timing of the examination; the fact that you should not start work until the signal and must stop work at a signal, etc. If there are any *special* instructions, such as a choice of questions to be answered, make sure that you note this instruction carefully.

2) When you are ready to start work on the examination, that is as soon as the signal has been given, read the instructions to each question booklet, underline any key words or phrases, such as *least*, *best*, *outline*, *describe* and the like. In this way you will tend to answer as requested rather than discover on reviewing your paper that you *listed without describing*, that you selected the *worst* choice rather than the *best* choice, etc.

3) If the examination is of the objective or multiple-choice type – that is, each question will also give a series of possible answers: A, B, C or D, and you are called upon to select the best answer and write the letter next to that answer on your answer paper – it is advisable to start answering each question in turn. There may be anywhere from 50 to 100 such questions in the three or four hours allotted and you can see how much time would be taken if you read through all the questions before beginning to answer any. Furthermore, if you come across a question or group of questions which you know would be difficult to answer, it would undoubtedly affect your handling of all the other questions.

4) If the examination is of the essay type and contains but a few questions, it is a moot point as to whether you should read all the questions before starting to answer any one. Of course, if you are given a choice – say five out of seven and the like – then it is essential to read all the questions so you can eliminate the two that are most difficult. If, however, you are asked to answer all the questions, there may be danger in trying to answer the easiest one first because you may find that you will spend too much time on it. The best technique is to answer the first question, then proceed to the second, etc.

5) Time your answers. Before the exam begins, write down the time it started, then add the time allowed for the examination and write down the time it must be completed, then divide the time available somewhat as follows:
   - If 3-1/2 hours are allowed, that would be 210 minutes. If you have 80 objective-type questions, that would be an average of 2-1/2 minutes per question. Allow yourself no more than 2 minutes per question, or a total of 160 minutes, which will permit about 50 minutes to review.
   - If for the time allotment of 210 minutes there are 7 essay questions to answer, that would average about 30 minutes a question. Give yourself only 25 minutes per question so that you have about 35 minutes to review.

6) The most important instruction is to *read each question* and make sure you know what is wanted. The second most important instruction is to *time yourself properly* so that you answer every question. The third most important instruction is to *answer every question.* Guess if you have to but include something for each question. Remember that you will receive no credit for a blank and will probably receive some credit if you write something in answer to an essay question. If you guess a letter – say "B" for a multiple-choice question – you may have guessed right. If you leave a blank as an answer to a multiple-choice question, the examiners may respect your feelings but it will not add a point to your score. Some exams may penalize you for wrong answers, so in such cases *only*, you may not want to guess unless you have some basis for your answer.

7) Suggestions
   a. Objective-type questions
      1. Examine the question booklet for proper sequence of pages and questions
      2. Read all instructions carefully
      3. Skip any question which seems too difficult; return to it after all other questions have been answered
      4. Apportion your time properly; do not spend too much time on any single question or group of questions

5. Note and underline key words – *all, most, fewest, least, best, worst, same, opposite,* etc.
6. Pay particular attention to negatives
7. Note unusual option, e.g., unduly long, short, complex, different or similar in content to the body of the question
8. Observe the use of "hedging" words – *probably, may, most likely,* etc.
9. Make sure that your answer is put next to the same number as the question
10. Do not second-guess unless you have good reason to believe the second answer is definitely more correct
11. Cross out original answer if you decide another answer is more accurate; do not erase until you are ready to hand your paper in
12. Answer all questions; guess unless instructed otherwise
13. Leave time for review

b. Essay questions
1. Read each question carefully
2. Determine exactly what is wanted. Underline key words or phrases.
3. Decide on outline or paragraph answer
4. Include many different points and elements unless asked to develop any one or two points or elements
5. Show impartiality by giving pros and cons unless directed to select one side only
6. Make and write down any assumptions you find necessary to answer the questions
7. Watch your English, grammar, punctuation and choice of words
8. Time your answers; don't crowd material

8) Answering the essay question

Most essay questions can be answered by framing the specific response around several key words or ideas. Here are a few such key words or ideas:

M's: manpower, materials, methods, money, management
P's: purpose, program, policy, plan, procedure, practice, problems, pitfalls, personnel, public relations

a. Six basic steps in handling problems:
1. Preliminary plan and background development
2. Collect information, data and facts
3. Analyze and interpret information, data and facts
4. Analyze and develop solutions as well as make recommendations
5. Prepare report and sell recommendations
6. Install recommendations and follow up effectiveness

b. Pitfalls to avoid
1. *Taking things for granted* – A statement of the situation does not necessarily imply that each of the elements is necessarily true; for example, a complaint may be invalid and biased so that all that can be taken for granted is that a complaint has been registered

2. *Considering only one side of a situation* – Wherever possible, indicate several alternatives and then point out the reasons you selected the best one
3. *Failing to indicate follow up* – Whenever your answer indicates action on your part, make certain that you will take proper follow-up action to see how successful your recommendations, procedures or actions turn out to be
4. *Taking too long in answering any single question* – Remember to time your answers properly

IX. AFTER THE TEST

Scoring procedures differ in detail among civil service jurisdictions although the general principles are the same. Whether the papers are hand-scored or graded by machine we have described, they are nearly always graded by number. That is, the person who marks the paper knows only the number – never the name – of the applicant. Not until all the papers have been graded will they be matched with names. If other tests, such as training and experience or oral interview ratings have been given, scores will be combined. Different parts of the examination usually have different weights. For example, the written test might count 60 percent of the final grade, and a rating of training and experience 40 percent. In many jurisdictions, veterans will have a certain number of points added to their grades.

After the final grade has been determined, the names are placed in grade order and an eligible list is established. There are various methods for resolving ties between those who get the same final grade – probably the most common is to place first the name of the person whose application was received first. Job offers are made from the eligible list in the order the names appear on it. You will be notified of your grade and your rank as soon as all these computations have been made. This will be done as rapidly as possible.

People who are found to meet the requirements in the announcement are called "eligibles." Their names are put on a list of eligible candidates. An eligible's chances of getting a job depend on how high he stands on this list and how fast agencies are filling jobs from the list.

When a job is to be filled from a list of eligibles, the agency asks for the names of people on the list of eligibles for that job. When the civil service commission receives this request, it sends to the agency the names of the three people highest on this list. Or, if the job to be filled has specialized requirements, the office sends the agency the names of the top three persons who meet these requirements from the general list.

The appointing officer makes a choice from among the three people whose names were sent to him. If the selected person accepts the appointment, the names of the others are put back on the list to be considered for future openings.

That is the rule in hiring from all kinds of eligible lists, whether they are for typist, carpenter, chemist, or something else. For every vacancy, the appointing officer has his choice of any one of the top three eligibles on the list. This explains why the person whose name is on top of the list sometimes does not get an appointment when some of the persons lower on the list do. If the appointing officer chooses the second or third eligible, the No. 1 eligible does not get a job at once, but stays on the list until he is appointed or the list is terminated.

X. HOW TO PASS THE INTERVIEW TEST

The examination for which you applied requires an oral interview test. You have already taken the written test and you are now being called for the interview test – the final part of the formal examination.

You may think that it is not possible to prepare for an interview test and that there are no procedures to follow during an interview. Our purpose is to point out some things you can do in advance that will help you and some good rules to follow and pitfalls to avoid while you are being interviewed.

What is an interview supposed to test?

The written examination is designed to test the technical knowledge and competence of the candidate; the oral is designed to evaluate intangible qualities, not readily measured otherwise, and to establish a list showing the relative fitness of each candidate – as measured against his competitors – for the position sought. Scoring is not on the basis of "right" and "wrong," but on a sliding scale of values ranging from "not passable" to "outstanding." As a matter of fact, it is possible to achieve a relatively low score without a single "incorrect" answer because of evident weakness in the qualities being measured.

Occasionally, an examination may consist entirely of an oral test – either an individual or a group oral. In such cases, information is sought concerning the technical knowledges and abilities of the candidate, since there has been no written examination for this purpose. More commonly, however, an oral test is used to supplement a written examination.

Who conducts interviews?

The composition of oral boards varies among different jurisdictions. In nearly all, a representative of the personnel department serves as chairman. One of the members of the board may be a representative of the department in which the candidate would work. In some cases, "outside experts" are used, and, frequently, a businessman or some other representative of the general public is asked to serve. Labor and management or other special groups may be represented. The aim is to secure the services of experts in the appropriate field.

However the board is composed, it is a good idea (and not at all improper or unethical) to ascertain in advance of the interview who the members are and what groups they represent. When you are introduced to them, you will have some idea of their backgrounds and interests, and at least you will not stutter and stammer over their names.

What should be done before the interview?

While knowledge about the board members is useful and takes some of the surprise element out of the interview, there is other preparation which is more substantive. It *is* possible to prepare for an oral interview – in several ways:

1) Keep a copy of your application and review it carefully before the interview

This may be the only document before the oral board, and the starting point of the interview. Know what education and experience you have listed there, and the sequence and dates of all of it. Sometimes the board will ask you to review the highlights of your experience for them; you should not have to hem and haw doing it.

2) Study the class specification and the examination announcement

Usually, the oral board has one or both of these to guide them. The qualities, characteristics or knowledges required by the position sought are stated in these documents. They offer valuable clues as to the nature of the oral interview. For example, if the job involves supervisory responsibilities, the announcement will usually indicate that knowledge of modern supervisory methods and the qualifications of the candidate as a supervisor will be tested. If so, you can expect such questions, frequently in the form of a hypothetical situation which you are expected to solve. NEVER go into an oral without knowledge of the duties and responsibilities of the job you seek.

3) Think through each qualification required

Try to visualize the kind of questions you would ask if you were a board member. How well could you answer them? Try especially to appraise your own knowledge and background in each area, *measured against the job sought*, and identify any areas in which you are weak. Be critical and realistic – do not flatter yourself.

4) Do some general reading in areas in which you feel you may be weak

For example, if the job involves supervision and your past experience has NOT, some general reading in supervisory methods and practices, particularly in the field of human relations, might be useful. Do NOT study agency procedures or detailed manuals. The oral board will be testing your understanding and capacity, not your memory.

5) Get a good night's sleep and watch your general health and mental attitude

You will want a clear head at the interview. Take care of a cold or any other minor ailment, and of course, no hangovers.

What should be done on the day of the interview?

Now comes the day of the interview itself. Give yourself plenty of time to get there. Plan to arrive somewhat ahead of the scheduled time, particularly if your appointment is in the fore part of the day. If a previous candidate fails to appear, the board might be ready for you a bit early. By early afternoon an oral board is almost invariably behind schedule if there are many candidates, and you may have to wait. Take along a book or magazine to read, or your application to review, but leave any extraneous material in the waiting room when you go in for your interview. In any event, relax and compose yourself.

The matter of dress is important. The board is forming impressions about you – from your experience, your manners, your attitude, and your appearance. Give your personal appearance careful attention. Dress your best, but not your flashiest. Choose conservative, appropriate clothing, and be sure it is immaculate. This is a business interview, and your appearance should indicate that you regard it as such. Besides, being well groomed and properly dressed will help boost your confidence.

Sooner or later, someone will call your name and escort you into the interview room. *This is it.* From here on you are on your own. It is too late for any more preparation. But remember, you asked for this opportunity to prove your fitness, and you are here because your request was granted.

What happens when you go in?

The usual sequence of events will be as follows: The clerk (who is often the board stenographer) will introduce you to the chairman of the oral board, who will introduce you to the other members of the board. Acknowledge the introductions before you sit down. Do not be surprised if you find a microphone facing you or a stenotypist sitting by. Oral interviews are usually recorded in the event of an appeal or other review.

Usually the chairman of the board will open the interview by reviewing the highlights of your education and work experience from your application – primarily for the benefit of the other members of the board, as well as to get the material into the record. Do not interrupt or comment unless there is an error or significant misinterpretation; if that is the case, do not hesitate. But do not quibble about insignificant matters. Also, he will usually ask you some question about your education, experience or your present job – partly to get you to start talking and to establish the interviewing "rapport." He may start the actual questioning, or turn it over to one of the other members. Frequently, each member undertakes the questioning on a particular area, one in which he is perhaps most competent, so you can expect each member to participate in the examination. Because time is limited, you may also expect some rather abrupt switches in the direction the questioning takes, so do not be upset by it. Normally, a board member will not pursue a single line of questioning unless he discovers a particular strength or weakness.

After each member has participated, the chairman will usually ask whether any member has any further questions, then will ask you if you have anything you wish to add. Unless you are expecting this question, it may floor you. Worse, it may start you off on an extended, extemporaneous speech. The board is not usually seeking more information. The question is principally to offer you a last opportunity to present further qualifications or to indicate that you have nothing to add. So, if you feel that a significant qualification or characteristic has been overlooked, it is proper to point it out in a sentence or so. Do not compliment the board on the thoroughness of their examination – they have been sketchy, and you know it. If you wish, merely say, "No thank you, I have nothing further to add." This is a point where you can "talk yourself out" of a good impression or fail to present an important bit of information. Remember, *you close the interview yourself.*

The chairman will then say, "That is all, Mr. _______, thank you." Do not be startled; the interview is over, and quicker than you think. Thank him, gather your belongings and take your leave. Save your sigh of relief for the other side of the door.

How to put your best foot forward

Throughout this entire process, you may feel that the board individually and collectively is trying to pierce your defenses, seek out your hidden weaknesses and embarrass and confuse you. Actually, this is not true. They are obliged to make an appraisal of your qualifications for the job you are seeking, and they want to see you in your best light. Remember, they must interview all candidates and a non-cooperative candidate may become a failure in spite of their best efforts to bring out his qualifications. Here are 15 suggestions that will help you:

1) Be natural – Keep your attitude confident, not cocky

If you are not confident that you can do the job, do not expect the board to be. Do not apologize for your weaknesses, try to bring out your strong points. The board is interested in a positive, not negative, presentation. Cockiness will antagonize any board member and make him wonder if you are covering up a weakness by a false show of strength.

2) Get comfortable, but don't lounge or sprawl

Sit erectly but not stiffly. A careless posture may lead the board to conclude that you are careless in other things, or at least that you are not impressed by the importance of the occasion. Either conclusion is natural, even if incorrect. Do not fuss with your clothing, a pencil or an ashtray. Your hands may occasionally be useful to emphasize a point; do not let them become a point of distraction.

3) Do not wisecrack or make small talk

This is a serious situation, and your attitude should show that you consider it as such. Further, the time of the board is limited – they do not want to waste it, and neither should you.

4) Do not exaggerate your experience or abilities

In the first place, from information in the application or other interviews and sources, the board may know more about you than you think. Secondly, you probably will not get away with it. An experienced board is rather adept at spotting such a situation, so do not take the chance.

5) If you know a board member, do not make a point of it, yet do not hide it

Certainly you are not fooling him, and probably not the other members of the board. Do not try to take advantage of your acquaintanceship – it will probably do you little good.

6) Do not dominate the interview

Let the board do that. They will give you the clues – do not assume that you have to do all the talking. Realize that the board has a number of questions to ask you, and do not try to take up all the interview time by showing off your extensive knowledge of the answer to the first one.

7) Be attentive

You only have 20 minutes or so, and you should keep your attention at its sharpest throughout. When a member is addressing a problem or question to you, give him your undivided attention. Address your reply principally to him, but do not exclude the other board members.

8) Do not interrupt

A board member may be stating a problem for you to analyze. He will ask you a question when the time comes. Let him state the problem, and wait for the question.

9) Make sure you understand the question

Do not try to answer until you are sure what the question is. If it is not clear, restate it in your own words or ask the board member to clarify it for you. However, do not haggle about minor elements.

10) Reply promptly but not hastily

A common entry on oral board rating sheets is "candidate responded readily," or "candidate hesitated in replies." Respond as promptly and quickly as you can, but do not jump to a hasty, ill-considered answer.

11) Do not be peremptory in your answers

A brief answer is proper – but do not fire your answer back. That is a losing game from your point of view. The board member can probably ask questions much faster than you can answer them.

12) Do not try to create the answer you think the board member wants

He is interested in what kind of mind you have and how it works – not in playing games. Furthermore, he can usually spot this practice and will actually grade you down on it.

13) Do not switch sides in your reply merely to agree with a board member

Frequently, a member will take a contrary position merely to draw you out and to see if you are willing and able to defend your point of view. Do not start a debate, yet do not surrender a good position. If a position is worth taking, it is worth defending.

14) Do not be afraid to admit an error in judgment if you are shown to be wrong

The board knows that you are forced to reply without any opportunity for careful consideration. Your answer may be demonstrably wrong. If so, admit it and get on with the interview.

15) Do not dwell at length on your present job

The opening question may relate to your present assignment. Answer the question but do not go into an extended discussion. You are being examined for a *new* job, not your present one. As a matter of fact, try to phrase ALL your answers in terms of the job for which you are being examined.

Basis of Rating

Probably you will forget most of these "do's" and "don'ts" when you walk into the oral interview room. Even remembering them all will not ensure you a passing grade. Perhaps you did not have the qualifications in the first place. But remembering them will help you to put your best foot forward, without treading on the toes of the board members.

Rumor and popular opinion to the contrary notwithstanding, an oral board wants you to make the best appearance possible. They know you are under pressure – but they also want to see how you respond to it as a guide to what your reaction would be under the pressures of the job you seek. They will be influenced by the degree of poise you display, the personal traits you show and the manner in which you respond.

ABOUT THIS BOOK

This book contains tests divided into Examination Sections. Go through each test, answering every question in the margin. We have also attached a sample answer sheet at the back of the book that can be removed and used. At the end of each test look at the answer key and check your answers. On the ones you got wrong, look at the right answer choice and learn. Do not fill in the answers first. Do not memorize the questions and answers, but understand the answer and principles involved. On your test, the questions will likely be different from the samples. Questions are changed and new ones added. If you understand these past questions you should have success with any changes that arise. Tests may consist of several types of questions. We have additional books on each subject should more study be advisable or necessary for you. Finally, the more you study, the better prepared you will be. This book is intended to be the last thing you study before you walk into the examination room. Prior study of relevant texts is also recommended. NLC publishes some of these in our Fundamental Series. Knowledge and good sense are important factors in passing your exam. Good luck also helps. So now study this Passbook, absorb the material contained within and take that knowledge into the examination. Then do your best to pass that exam.

EXAMINATION SECTION

EXAMINATION SECTION

TEST 1

DIRECTIONS: Each question or incomplete statement is followed by several suggested answers or completions. Select the one that BEST answers the question or completes the statement. *PRINT THE LETTER OF THE CORRECT ANSWER IN THE SPACE AT THE RIGHT.*

1. The Donaldson Company's cash balance includes a sum of $1,200,000 appropriated by the Board of Directors for the purchase of new equipment. On its financial statements, this amount should be included on the 1.____
   A. balance sheet as a current asset
   B. balance sheet as a non-current asset, specifically identified
   C. balance sheet as a fixed asset, included as part of plant cost
   D. income statement as a non-operating expense

2. The trial balance of the Davis Corporation as of June 30, 2021, the end of its fiscal year, included opposite the title ESTIMATED FEDERAL INCOME TAXES ACCRUED the amount of $35,000, which included the company's estimate of the Federal income tax it would have to pay for its 2021 fiscal year and the amount of an unpaid additional assessment for the 2018 fiscal year. This amount should appear on the balance sheet as a(n) 2.____
   A. general reserve
   B. reduction of current assets
   C. current liability
   D. allocation of retained income

3. A weekly payroll check was issued to an hourly employee based upon 88 hours of work instead of the normal 38 hours. The time card was somewhat illegible, and the number looked like it could have been 88. The BEST control procedure to prevent such an error would be 3.____
   A. desk checking
   B. a hash total
   C. a limit test
   D. a code check

4. In preparing a bank reconciliation, outstanding checks should be 4.____
   A. *deducted* from the balance per books
   B. *deducted* from the balance per bank statement
   C. *added* to the balance per books
   D. *added* to the balance per bank statement

5. Independence is essential and is expected under the generally accepted auditing standards. The face and appearance of integrity and objectivity are BEST maintained if 5.____
   A. the auditor is unbiased
   B. the auditor is aware of the problem of third party liability
   C. there is no financial relationship between the client and the auditor
   D. all financial relationships between the auditor and the client are reported in footnote form

6. An audit program is a plan of action and is used to guide the auditor in planning his work. 6.____
Such a program, if standardized, must be modified to
   A. observe limits that management places on the audit
   B. counteract internal control weaknesses
   C. meet the limited training of the auditor
   D. limit interference with work of the firm being audited

7. In auditing the *Owner's Equity* section of any company, the section related to a publicly-held corporation which uses a transfer agent and registrar would be more intricate than the audit of a partnership. 7.____
Therefore, the procedure that an auditor should use in this case is to
   A. obtain a listing of the number of shares of securities outstanding
   B. make a count of the number of shareholders
   C. determine that all stock transfers have been properly handled
   D. count the number of shares of stock in the treasury

8. In recent years, it has become increasingly more important to determine the correct number of shares outstanding when auditing the owner's equity accounts. 8.____
This is TRUE because
   A. there has been more fraud with respect to securities issued
   B. there are increased complexities determining the earnings per share
   C. there are more large corporations
   D. the auditor has to test the amount of invested capital

9. In auditing corporation records, an auditor must refer to some corporate documents that are not accounting documents. 9.____
The one of the following to which he is LEAST likely to refer is
   A. minutes of the board of directors meeting
   B. articles of incorporation of the corporation
   C. correspondence with public relations firms and the shareholders
   D. the by-laws of the corporation

10. A generally accepted auditing procedure which has been required by AICPA requirements is the observation of inventories. 10.____
Since it is impossible to observe the entire inventory of a large firm, the auditor may satisfy this requirement by
   A. establishing the balance by the use of a gross profit percentage method
   B. using sampling procedures to verify the count made by the client
   C. accepting the perpetual inventory records, once he has established that the entries are arithmetically accurate
   D. accepting the management statement that the inventory is correct as to quantity where observation is difficult

11. Materiality is an important consideration in all aspects of an audit examination. 11.____
Attention must be given to accounts with small and zero balances when examining accounts payable.
This does not conflict with the concept of materiality because

A. The size of a balance is no clue to possible understatement of a liability
B. the balance of the account is not a measure of materiality
C. a sampling technique may suggest examining those accounts under consideration
D. the total of the accounts payable may be a material amount and, therefore, no individual account payable should be eliminated from review

12. In establishing the amount of a liability recorded on the books, which of the following types of evidence should an auditor consider to be the MOST reliable? 12.____
A. A check issued by the company and bearing the payee's endorsement which is included with the bank statement
B. Confirmation of an account payable balance mailed by and returned directly to the auditor
C. A sales invoice issued by the client with a delivery receipt from an outside trucker attached
D. A working paper prepared by the client's accountant and reviewed by the client's controller

13. Prior period adjustments as defined by APIB Opinion #9 issued by the AICPA never flow through the income statement. 13.____
The one of the following which is NOT one of the four criteria established b APB #9 for meeting the qualifications for treatment as a prior period adjustment is that the adjustment item
A. is not susceptible to reasonable extension prior to the current period
B. must be determined primarily by someone other than company management
C. can be specifically identified with and directly related to the business activities of a particular prior period
D. when placed in the current period would give undesirable results of operations

14. The subject caption which does NOT belong in a report of a financial audit and review of operations of public agency is 14.____
A. Audit Program
B. Description of Agency Organization and Function
C. Summary Statement of Findings
D. Details of Findings

15. At the inception of an audit of a public assistance agency, you ascertain that the one-year period of your audit includes 240,000 serially numbered payment vouchers. 15.____
The sample selection which would enable you to render the MOST generally acceptable opinion on the number of ineligible persons receiving public assistance is
A. the number of vouchers issued in a one-month period
B. every hundredth voucher
C. a random statistical selection
D. an equal size block of vouchers from each month

16. Of the following, the one which BEST describes an internal control system is the 16.____
   A. division of the handling and recording of each transaction into component parts so as to involve at least two persons, with each performing an unduplicated part of each transaction
   B. expansion of the worksheet to include provisions for adjustments to the books of account prior to preparation of the financial statements
   C. recording of transactions affecting negotiable instruments in accordance with the principles of debit and credit, and giving these instruments special treatment if they are interest or non-interest bearing notes
   D. taking of discounts, when properly authorized by the vendor, as an incentive for prompt payment

17. During audits of small businesses, an accountant is less likely to find that these establishments have a system of internal control comparable to larger firms because small businesses GENERALLY 17.____
   A. can absorb the cost of small fraudulent acts which may be perpetrated
   B. benefit more than larger firms by prevention of fraud than by detection of fraud
   C. have limited staff and the costs of maintaining the system are high
   D. use a double entry system which serves as a substitute for internal control

18. In the performance of a financial audit, especially one where there is a need for a thorough knowledge of law, an accountant would BEST be advised to 18.____
   A. rely on the testimony of witnesses, as they may be found during the course of the audit, in preference to the written record
   B. rely on the presumption that the client's actions are illegal when the audit discloses meager facts or evidence
   C. be aware of the specific legal objectives he is attempting to attain by means of his audit
   D. be aware of different conclusions he can reach depending upon what facts are stressed or discounted in his audit

19. There are various types of budgets which are used to measure different government activities. 19.____
   The type of budget which PARTICULARLY measures input of resource as compared with output service is the _____ budget.
   A. capital B. traditional C. performance D. program

20. Bank balances are usually confirmed through the use of a standard bank confirmation form as authorized by the AICPA and the Bank Administration Institute. 20.____
   In addition to bank balances, these confirmations ALSO confirm
   A. the credit rating of the client
   B. details of all deposits during the past month
   C. loans and contingent liabilities outstanding
   D. securities held by the bank as custodian or the client

KEY (CORRECT ANSWERS)

1.	B	11.	A
2.	C	12.	B
3.	C	13.	D
4.	B	14.	A
5.	C	15.	C
6.	B	16.	A
7.	A	17.	C
8.	B	18.	C
9.	C	19.	C
10.	B	20.	C

TEST 2

DIRECTIONS: Each question or incomplete statement is followed by several suggested answers or completions. Select the one that BEST answers the question or completes the statement. *PRINT THE LETTER OF THE CORRECT ANSWER IN THE SPACE AT THE RIGHT.*

Questions 1-3.

DIRECTIONS: Questions 1 through 3 are based on the classification of items into the appropriate section of a corporation balance sheet. The list of sections to be used is given below:

Current Assets	Investments
Current Liabilities	Long-term Liabilities
Deferred Credits	Paid-in Capital
Deferred Expenses	Plant Assets
Intangible assets	Retained Earnings

1. With respect to *Bonds Payable Due* in 2021, the PROPER classification is 1.____
   A. Investments B. Paid-in Capital
   C. Retained Earnings D. Long-term Liabilities

2. With respect to *Premium on Common Stock*, the PROPER classification is 2.____
   A. Intangible Assets B. Investments
   C. Retained Earnings D. Paid-in Capital

3. With respect to *Organization Costs,* the PROPER classification is 3.____
   A. Intangible Assets B. Investments
   C. Plant Assets D. Current Liabilities

4. J. Frost operates a small, individually owned repair service and maintains adequate double entry records. A review of his bank accounts and other available financial records yields the following information: 4.____
   Deposits made during 2021 per bank statements totaled $360,000. Deposits included a bank loan of $25,000 and an additional investment by Frost of $5,000. Disbursements during 2021 per bank statements totaled $305,000. This amount includes personal withdrawals of $28,500 and repayment of debt of $15,000.
   The Net Equity of J. Frost at January 1, 2021 was determined to be $61,000. Net Equity of J. Frost at December 31, 2021 was determined to be $67,000. Based upon the *Net Worth* method, Frost's net income for the year ended December 31, 2021 was
   A. $6,000 B. $29,500 C. $41,500 D. $55,000

Questions 5-8.

DIRECTIONS: Questions 5 through 8 are based on the following Balance Sheet, Income statement, and Notes relating to the books and records of the Hartman Corporation.

BALANCE SHEET (000 omitted)

	September 30, 2020 Debit	September 30, 2020 Credit	September 30, 2021 Debit	September 30, 2021 Credit
Cash	$18		$31	
Accounts Receivable	28		26	
Inventory	10		15	
Land	40		81	
Building and equipment (Net)	60		65	
Accounts Payable		$10		$11
Notes Payable		2		2
Bonds Payable		50		50
Mortgage Payable		20		46
Common Stock		50		86
Retained Earnings		24		23
	$156	$156	$218	$218

INCOME STATEMENT FOR FISCAL YEAR ENDING SEPTEMBER 30, 2021

Income:		
Sales		$85
Cost of Sales		40
Gross Margin		$45
Expenses:		
Depreciation	$5	
Loss on Sale of Fixed Assets	2	
Other Operating Expenses	32	
Total Expenses		$39
Net Income		$6

NOTES:

1. Dividend declared during the year 2021, $7,000
2. Acquired land; gave $36,000 common stock and cash for the balance.
3. Wrote off $1,000 accounts receivable and as uncollectible.
4. Acquired equipment; gave note secured by mortgage of $26,000.
5. Sold equipment; net cost per books, $16,000, sales price $14,000.

5. The amount of funds provided from net income for the year ended September 30 2021 is 5.____

   A. $6,000 B. $7,000 C. $13,000 D. $14,000

6. Financing and investing activities not affecting working capital are reported under the rules of APB #19. Notes 1 through 5 refer to various transactions on the books of the Hartman Corporation. 6.____
   Select the answer which refers to the numbers reflecting the concept mentioned here.

   A. Notes 1, 3, and 5
   B. Notes 2 and 4
   C. Notes 2, 4, and 5
   D. All five notes

7. Funds applied for the acquisition of the land are 7.____
   A. $5,000 B. $36,000 C. $41,000 D. None

8. The net change in working capital from 2020 to 2021 is 8.____
   A. $6,000 B. $16,000 C. $22,000 D. $35,000

9. Sales during July 2021 for the Magnum Corporation, operating in Los Angeles, were $378,000, of which $150,000 were on account. The sales figures given include the total sales tax charged to retail customers. (Assume a sales tax rate on all sales of 8%.) 9.____
   The CORRECT sales tax liability for July 2021 should be shown as
   A. $3,024 B. $18,240 C. $28,000 D. $30,240

10. Of the following statement ratios, the one that BEST represents a measure of cost efficiency is 10.____
    A. Acid Test Ratio
    B. Operating Costs to Net Sales Ratio
    C. Cost of Manufacturing to Plant Assets Radio
    D. Earnings Per Share

Questions 11-13.

DIRECTIONS: Questions 11 through 13 are to be answered on the basis of the following information:

An examination of the books and records of the Kay May Corporation, a machinery wholesaler, reveals the following facts for the year ended December 31, 2021:

a. Merchandise was sold and billed F.O.B. shipping point on December 31, 2021 at a sales price of $7,500. Although the merchandise costing $6,000 was ready for shipment on that date, the trucking company did not call for the merchandise until January 2, 2022. It was not included in the inventory count taken on December 31, 2021.
b. Merchandise with a sales price of $5,500 was billed and shipped to the customer on December 31, 2021. The merchandise costing $4,800 was not included in the inventory count taken on that day. Terms of sale were F.O.B. destination.
c. Merchandise costing $5,000 was recorded as a purchase on December 26, 2021. The merchandise was not included in the inventory count taken on December 31, 2021 since, upon examination, it was found to be defective and was in the process of being returned to the vendor.
d. Merchandise costing $2,500 was received on December 31, 2021. It was included in the inventory count on that date. Although the invoice was dated January 3, 2022, the purchase was recorded in the December 2021 Purchases Journal.
e. Merchandise costing $4,000 was received on January 3, 2022. It was shipped F.O.B. destination, and the invoice was dated December 30, 2021. The invoice was recorded in the December 2021 Purchases Journal, and the merchandise was included in the December 31, 2021 inventory.

11. The net change to correct the inventory value as of December 31, 2021 is: 11.____
    A. Increase $800 B. Increase $5,800
    C. Increase $6,800 D. Decrease $12,055

12. The net change to correct the sales figure for the year 2021 is: 12.____
    A. Increase $2,000 B. Decrease $5,500
    C. Decrease $7,500 D. $13,000

13. The net change to correct the purchases figure for the year 2021 is: 13.____
    A. Decrease $11,500 B. Decrease $4,000
    C. Decrease $5,000 D. Decrease $9,000

Questions 14-18.

DIRECTIONS: Each of the following Questions 14 through 18 consists of a description of a transaction that indicates a two-fold effect on the Balance Sheet. Each of these transactions may be classified under one of the following categories:

A. Assets are Understated, Retained Earnings are Understated
B. Assets are Overstated, Retained Earnings are Overstated
C. Liabilities are Understated, Retained Earnings are Overstated
D. Liabilities are Overstated, Retained Earnings are Understated

Examine each question carefully. In the correspondingly numbered space at the right, print the letter preceding the category above which BEST describes the effect of each transaction on the Balance Sheet as of December 31, 2021.

14. A major equipment purchase was made at the beginning of 2021. The equipment had an estimated six-year useful life, and depreciation was overlooked at December 31, 2021. 14.____

15. Unearned Rental Income was properly credited when received early in the year. No year-end adjustment was made to transfer the earned portion to an appropriate account. 15.____

16. Goods on hand at a branch office were excluded from the year-end physical inventory. The purchase of these goods had been properly recorded 16.____

17. Accrued Interest on Notes Receivable was overlooked as of December 31, 2021. 17.____

18. Accrued Federal Income Taxes for 2021 have never been recorded. 18.____

19. The following are account balances for the dates shown: 19.____

	Dec. 31, 2021	Dec. 31, 2020
Current Assets:		
Cash	$168,000	$60,000
Short-term investments	16,000	20,000
Accounts receivable (net)	160,000	100,000
Inventory	60,000	40,000
Prepaid expenses	4,000	40,000
Current Liabilities:		
Accounts payable	110,000	80,000
Dividends payable	30,000	0

Given the above account balances, the CHANGE in working capital is a(n)
A. increase of $128,000
B. decrease of $128,000
C. increase of $188,000
D. decrease of $188,000

20. In conducting an audit of plant assets, which of the following accounts MUST be examined in order to ascertain that additions to plant assets have been correctly stated and reflect charges that are properly capitalized? 20.____
A. Accounts receivable
B. Sales income
C. Maintenance and repairs
D. Investments

KEY (CORRECT ANSWERS)

1.	D	11.	A
2.	D	12.	B
3.	A	13.	D
4.	B	14.	B
5.	C	15.	D
6.	B	16.	A
7.	A	17.	A
8.	B	18.	C
9.	C	19.	A
10.	B	20.	C

EXAMINATION SECTION

TEST 1

DIRECTIONS: Each question or incomplete statement is followed by several suggested answers or completions. Select the one that BEST answers the question or completes the statement. *PRINT THE LETTER OF THE CORRECT ANSWER IN THE SPACE AT THE RIGHT.*

1. Gross income of an individual for Federal income tax purposes does NOT include 1.____
   A. interest credited to a bank savings account
   B. gain from the sale of sewer authority bonds
   C. back pay received as a result of job reinstatement
   D. interest received from State Dormitory Authority bonds

2. A cash-basis, calendar-year taxpayer purchased an annuity policy at a total cost of $20,000. Starting on January 1 of 2022, he began to receive annual payments of $1,500. His life expectancy as of that date was 16 years. The amount of annuity income to be included in his gross income for the taxable year 2022 is 2.____
   A. none B. $250 C. $1,250 D. $1,500

3. The transactions related to a municipal police retirement system should be included in a(n) _____ fund. 3.____
   A. intra-governmental service B. trust
   C. general D. special revenue

4. The budget for a given cost during a given period was $100,000. The actual cost for the period was $90,000. Based upon these facts, one should say that the responsible manager has done a better than expected job in controlling the cost if the cost is _____ budgeted production. 4.____
   A. variable and actual production equaled
   B. a discretionary fixed cost and actual production equaled
   C. variable and actual production was 90% of
   D. variable and actual production was 80% of

5. In the conduct of an audit, the MOST practical method by which an accountant can satisfy himself as to the physical existence of inventory is to 5.____
   A. be present and observe personally the audited firm's physical inventory being taken
   B. independently verify an adequate proportion of all inventory operations performed by the audited firm
   C. mail confirmation requests to vendors of merchandise sold to the audited firm within the inventory year
   D. review beforehand the adequacy of the audited firm's plan for inventory taking, and during the actual inventory-taking states, verify that this plan is being followed

Questions 6-7.

DIRECTIONS: Questions 6 and 7 are to be answered on the basis of the following information.

For the month of March, the ABC Manufacturing Corporation's estimated factory overhead for an expected volume of 15,000 lbs. of a product was as follows:

	Amount	Overhead Rate Per Unit
Fixed Overhead	$3,000	$.20
Variable Overhead	$9,000	$.60

Actual volume was 10,000 lbs. and actual overhead expense was $7,700.

6. The Spending (Budget) Variance was _____ (Favorable). 6.____
   A. $1,300 B. $6,000 C. $7,700 D. $9,000

7. The Idle Capacity Variance was 7.____
   A. $300 (Favorable) B. $1,000 (Unfavorable)
   C. $1,300 (Favorable) D. $8,000 (Unfavorable)

Questions 8-11.

DIRECTIONS: Questions 8 through 11 are to be answered on the basis of the following information.

A bookkeeper, who was not familiar with proper accounting procedures, prepared the following financial report for Largor Corporation as of December 31, 2021. In addition to the errors in presentation, additional data below was not considered in the preparation of the report. Restate this balance sheet in proper form, giving recognition to the additional data, so that you will be able to determine the required information to answer Questions 8 through 11.

LARGOR CORPORATION
December 31, 2021

Current Assets			
Cash		$110,000	
Marketable Securities		53,000	
Accounts Receivable	$261,400		
Accounts Payable	125,000	136,400	
Inventories		274,000	
Prepaid Expenses		24,000	
Treasury Stock		20,000	
Cash Surrender Value of Officers' Life Insurance Policies		105,000	$722,400
Plant Assets			
Equipment		350,000	
Building	200,000		
Reserve for Plant Expansion	75,000	125,000	
Land		47,500	
TOTAL ASSETS			$1,244,900

Liabilities			
Salaries Payable		16,500	
Cash Dividend Payable		50,000	
Stock Dividend Payable		70,000	
Bonds Payable	200,000		
Less Sinking Fund	90,000	110,000	
TOTAL LIABILITIES			$246,500
Stockholders' Equity:			
Paid In Capital			
Common Stock		350,000	
Retained Earnings and Reserves			
Reserve for Income Taxes	90,000		
Reserve for Doubtful Accounts	6,500		
Reserve for Treasury Stock	20,000		
Reserve for Depreciation Equipment	70,000		
Reserve for Depreciation Building	80,000		
Premium on Common Stock	15,000		
Retained Earnings	366,900	648,400	998,400
TOTAL LIABILITIES & EQUITY			1,244,900

Additional Data

A. Bond Payable will mature eight (8) years from Balance Sheet date.
B. The Stock Dividend Payable was declared on December 31, 2021.
C. The Reserve for Income Taxes represents the balance due on the estimated liability for taxes on income for the year ended December 31.
D. Advances from Customers at the Balance Sheet date totaled $13,600. This total is still credited against Accounts Receivable.
E. Prepaid Expenses include Unamortized Mortgage Costs of $15,000.
F. Marketable Securities were recorded at cost. Their market value at December 31, 2021 was $50,800.

8. After restatement of the balance sheet in proper form and giving recognition to the additional data, the Total Current Assets should be 8.____
A. $597,400 B. $702,400 C. $712,300 D. $827,300

9. After restatement of the balance sheet in proper form and giving recognition to the additional data, the Total Current Liabilities should be 9.____
A. $261,500 B. $281,500 C. $295,100 D. $370,100

10. After restatement of the balance sheet in proper form and giving recognition to the additional data, the net book value of plant and equipment should be 10.____
A. $400,000 B. $447,500 C. $550,000 D. $597,500

11. After restatement of the balance sheet in proper form and giving recognition to the additional data, the Stockholders Equity should be 11.____
A. $320,000 B. $335,000 C. $764,700 D. $874,700

12. When preparing the financial statement, dividends in arrears on preferred stock should be treated as a 12.____
   A. contingent liability
   B. deduction from capital
   C. parenthetical remark
   D. valuation reserve

13. The IPC Corporation has an intangible asset which it values at $1,000,000 and has a life expectancy of 60 years. 13.____
   The appropriate span of write-off, as determined by good accounting practice, should be _____ years.
   A. 17
   B. 34
   C. 40
   D. 60

14. The following information was used in costing inventory on October 31: 14.____

October	1 -	Beginning inventory	800 units	@ $1.20
	4 -	Received	200 units	@ $1.40
	16 -	Issued	400 units	
	24 -	Received	200 units	@ $1.60
	27 -	Issued	500 units	

   Using the LIFO method of inventory evaluation (end-of-month method), the total dollar value of the inventory at October 31 was
   A. $360
   B. $460
   C. $600
   D. $1,200

15. If a $400,000 par value bond issue paying 8%, with interest dates of June 30 and December 31, is sold in November 1 for par plus accrued interest, the cash proceeds received by the issuer on November 1 should be APPROXIMATELY 15.____
   A. $405,000
   B. $408,000
   C. $411,000
   D. $416,000

16. The TOTAL interest cost to the issuer of a bond issue sold for more than its face value is the periodic interest payment _____ amortization. 16.____
   A. plus the discount
   B. plus the premium
   C. minus the discount
   D. minus the premium

17. If shareholders donate shares of stock back to the company, such stock received by the company is properly classified as 17.____
   A. Treasury stock
   B. Unissued stock
   C. Other assets – investment
   D. Current assets - investment

18. Assume the following transactions have occurred: 18.____
   1. 10,000 shares of capital stock of Omer Corp., par value $50, have been sold and issued on initial sale @ $55 per share during the month of June
   2. 2,000 shares of previously issued stock were purchased from shareholders during the month of September @ $58 per share.

   As of September 30, the stockholders' equity section TOTAL should be
   A. $434,000
   B. $450,000
   C. $480,000
   D. $550,000

19. Mr. Diak, a calendar-year taxpayer in the construction business, agrees to construct a building for the Supermat Corporation to cost a total of $500,000 and to require about two years to complete. By December 31, 2021, he has expended $150,000 in costs, and it was determined that the building was 35% completed. 19.____
If Mr. Diak is reporting income under the completed contract method, the amount of gross income he will report for 2021 is
A. none B. $25,000 C. $175,000 D. $350,000

20. When the Board of Directors of a firm uses the present-value technique to aid in deciding whether or not to buy a new plant asset, it needs to have information reflecting 20.____
A. the cost of the new asset only
B. the increased production from use of new asset only
C. an estimated rate of return
D. the book value of the asset

KEY (CORRECT ANSWERS)

1.	D	11.	D
2.	B	12.	C
3.	B	13.	C
4.	A	14.	A
5.	D	15.	C
6.	A	16.	D
7.	B	17.	A
8.	C	18.	A
9.	C	19.	A
10.	B	20.	C

TEST 2

DIRECTIONS: Each question or incomplete statement is followed by several suggested answers or completions. Select the one that BEST answers the question or completes the statement. *PRINT THE LETTER OF THE CORRECT ANSWER IN THE SPACE AT THE RIGHT.*

Questions 1-3.

DIRECTIONS: Questions 1 through 3 are to be answered on the basis of the following information.

During your audit of the Avon Company, you find the following errors in the records of the company:

1. Incorrect exclusion from the final inventory of items costing $3,000 for which the purchase was not recorded.
2. Inclusion in the final inventory of goods costing $5,000, although a purchase was not recorded. The goods in question were being held on consignment from Reldrey Company.
3. Incorrect exclusion of $2,000 from the inventory count at the end of the period. The goods were in transit (F.O.B. shipping point); the invoice had been received and the purchase recorded.
4. Inclusion of items on the receiving dock that were being held for return to the vendor because of damage. In counting the goods in the receiving department, these items were incorrectly included. With respect to these goods, a purchase of $4,000 had been recorded.

The records (uncorrected) showed the following amounts:
1. Purchases, $170,000
2. Pretax income, $15,000
3. Accounts payable, $20,000; and
4. Inventory at the end of the period, $40,000.

1. The CORRECTED inventory is 1.____
   A. $36,000 B. $42,000 C. $43,000 D. $44,000

2. The CORRECTED income for the year is 2.____
   A. $12,000 B. $15,000 C. $17,000 D. $18,000

3. The CORRECT accounts payable liabilities are 3.____
   A. $16,000 B. $17,000 C. $19,000 D. $23,000

4. An auditing procedure that is MOST likely to reveal the existence of a contingent liability is 4.____
   A. a review of vouchers paid during the month following the year end
   B. confirmation of accounts payable
   C. an inquiry directed to legal counsel
   D. confirmation of mortgage notes

Questions 5-6.

DIRECTIONS: Questions 5 and 6 are to be answered on the basis of the following information.

Mr. Zelev operates a business as a sole proprietor and uses the cash basis for reporting income for income tax purposes. His bank account during 2021 for the business shows receipts totaling $285,000 and cash payments totaling $240,000. Included in the cash payments were payments for three-year business insurance policies whose premiums totaled $1,575. It was determined that the expired premiums for this year were $475. Further examination of the accounts and discussion with Mr. Zelev revealed the fact that included in the receipts were the following items, as well as the proceeds received from customers:

$15,000 which Mr. Zelev took from his savings account and deposited in the business account.

$20,000 which Mr. Zelev received from the bank as a loan which will be repaid next year.

Included in the cash payments were $10,000, which Mr. Zelev took on a weekly basis from the business receipts to use for his personal expenses.

5. The amount of net income to be reported for income tax purposes for calendar year 2022 for Mr. Zelev is 5.____
   A. $21,100 B. $26,100 C. $31,100 D. $46,100

6. Assuming the same facts as those reported above, Mr. Zelev would be required to pay a self-employment tax for 2022 of 6.____
   $895.05 B. $1,208.70 C. $1,234.35 D. $1,666.90

7. For the year ended December 2021, you are given the following information relative to the income and expense statements for the Sungam Manufacturers, Inc.: 7.____

Sales..	$1,000.000
Sales Returns...	95,000

Cost of Sales	
Opening Inventories	$200,000
Purchases During the Year	567,000
Direct Labor Costs	240,000
Factory Overhead	24,400
Inventories End of Year	235,000

On June 5, 2021, a fire destroyed the plant and all of the inventories then on hand. You are given the following information and asked to ascertain the amount of the estimated inventory loss.

Sales up to June 15	$545,000
Purchased to June 15	254,500
Direct Labor	233,000
Overhead	14,550
Salvaged Inventory	95,000

The ESTIMATED inventory loss is
A. $96,000 B. $162,450 C. $189,450 D. $257,450

8. Losses and excessive costs with regard to inventory can occur in any one of several operating functions of an organization.
The operating function which bears the GREATEST responsibility for the failure to give proper consideration to transportation costs of material acquisitions is 8.____
A. accounting B. purchasing C. receiving D. shipping

Questions 9-17.

DIRECTIONS: Questions 9 through 17 are to be answered on the basis of the following information.

You are conducting an audit of the PAP Company, which has a contract to supply the municipal hospitals with specialty refrigerators on a cost-plus basis. The following information is available:

Materials Purchased	$1,946,700
Inventories, January 1	
Materials	268,000
Finished Goods (100 units)	43,000
Direct Labor	2,125,800
Factory Overhead (40% variable)	764,000
Marketing Expenses (all fixed)	516,000
Administrative Expenses (all fixed)	461,000
Sales (12,400 units)	6,634,000
Inventories, March 31	
Materials	167,000
Finished Goods (200 units)	(omitted)
No Work in Process	

9. The NET INCOME for the period is 9.____
A. $755,500 B. $1,237,500 C. $1,732,500 D. $4,980,500

10. The number of units manufactured is 10.____
A. 12,400 B. 12,500 C. 12,600 D. 12,700

11. The unit cost of refrigerators manufactured is MOST NEARLY 11.____
A. $389.00 B. $395.00 C. $398.00 D. $400.00

12. The TOTAL variable costs are 12.____
A. $305,600 B. $464,000 C. $4,479,100 D. $4,937,500

13. The TOTAL fixed costs are 13.____
A. $458,400 B. $1,435,400 C. $1,471,800 D. $1,741,000

While you are conducting your audit, the PAP Company advises you that they have changed their inventory costing from FIFO to LIFO. You are interested in pursuing the matter further because this change will affect the cost of the refrigerators. An examination of material part 2-317 inventory card shows the following activity:

May 2 – Received 100 units @ $5.40 per unit
May 8 – Received 30 units @ $8.00 per unit
May 15 – Issued 50 units
May 22 – Received 120 units @ $9.00 per unit
May 29 – Issued 100 units

14. Using the FIFO method under a perpetual inventory control system, the TOTAL cost of the units issued in May is 14.____
    A. $690 B. $960 C. $1,590 D. $1,860

15. Using the FIFO method under a perpetual inventory control system, the VALUE of the closing inventory is 15.____
    A. $780 B. $900 C. $1,080 D. $1,590

16. Using the LIFO method under a perpetual inventory control system, the TOTAL cost of the units issued in May is 16.____
    A. $1,248 B. $1,428 C. $1,720 D. $1,860

17. Using the LIFO method under a perpetual inventory control system, the value of the closing inventory is 17.____
    A. $612 B. $380 C. $1,512 D. $1,680

Questions 18-20.

DIRECTIONS: For Questions 18 through 20, consider that the EEF Corporation has a fully integrated cost accounting system.

18. Unit cost of manufacturing dresses was $7.00. Spoiled dresses numbered 400 with a sales value of $800.
    When it is not customary to have a Spoiled Work account, the MOST appropriate account to be credited is 18.____
    A. Work in Process B. Cost of Sales
    C. Manufacturing Overhead D. Finished Goods

19. Overtime premium for factory workers (direct labor) totaled $400 for the payroll period. This was due to inadequate plant capacity.
    The account to be DEBITED is 19.____
    A. Work in Process B. Cost of Sales
    C. Manufacturing Overhead D. Finished Goods

20. A month-end physical inventory of stores shows a shortage of $175. The account to be DEBITED to correct this shortage is 20.____
    A. Stores
    B. Work in Process
    C. Cost of Sales
    D. Manufacturing Overhead

KEY (CORRECT ANSWERS)

1.	A	11.	B
2.	A	12.	C
3.	C	13.	B
4.	C	14.	B
5.	A	15.	B
6.	D	16.	A
7.	B	17.	A
8.	B	18.	A
9.	A	19.	C
10.	B	20.	C

ACCOUNTING

EXAMINATION SECTION
TEST 1

DIRECTIONS : Each question or incomplete statement is followed by several suggested answers or completions. Select the one that *BEST* answers the question or completes the statement. *PRINT THE LETTER OF THE CORRECT ANSWER IN THE SPACE AT THE RIGHT.*

Questions 1-5.

DIRECTIONS: Assume that you are requested to verify certain financial data with respect to the various business entities described below. This information is required to verify that tax returns and/or other financial reports submitted to your agency are correct.

In an auditing review of the income statements of several business firms (Companies X, Y, and Z), you find the financial information given below. Based upon the account balances shown, select the correct answer for the statement information requested.

Company X -	Sales	$ 160,000
	Opening Inventory	$ 70,000
	Purchases	$ 80,000
	Purchase Returns	$ 1,200
	Cost of Goods Sold	$ 127,000

1. The ending inventory based upon the data above is 1.____

   A. $21,800 B. $23,000 C. $24,200 D. $33,000

Company Y -	Opening Inventory	$ 50,000
	Purchases	$ 145,000
	Ending Inventory	$ 28,500
	Gross Profit	$ 56,000
	Sales and Administrative Expenses	$ 64,000

2. Sales for the period based upon the data above are 2.____

   A. $110,500 B. $166,500 C. $222,500 D. $286,500

Company Z -	Sales for the period	$ 200,000
	Net Profit	7% of Sales
	Purchases	$ 180,000
	Ending Inventory	$ 70,000
	Gross Profit	$ 60,000

3. Cost of Goods sold for Company Z is 3.____

   A. $110,000 B. $140,000 C. $180,000 D. $250,000

4. The opening inventory of Company Z would be 4.____

   A. $10,000 B. $20,000 C. $30,000 D. $80,000

5. The operating expenses for Company Z would be 5.____

   A. $10,000 B. $14,000 C. $20,000 D. $46,000

Questions 6-8.

DIRECTIONS: The following information is taken from the books and records of a business firm:

Sales for the calendar year 2018:	$52,000
<u>Based upon FIFO Inventory</u>:	
Good available for Sale	$46,900
Inventory at December 31, 2018	$12,700
<u>Based upon LIFO Inventory</u>:	
Goods available for Sale	$46,900
Inventory at December 31, 2018	$10,400

6. If FIFO Inventory valuation is used, the Gross Profit will be 6.____

A. $5,100 B. $15,500 C. $17,800 D. $34,200

7. If LIFO Inventory valuation method is used, the Gross Profit will be 7.____

A. $2,300 B. $15,500 C. $17,800 D. $36,500

8. If LIFO Inventory method is used, compared with the FIFO method, the cost of goods sold will be 8.____

A. more by $2,300
B. less by $2,300
C. more by $10,400
D. less by $12,700

9. Which one of the following would NOT properly be classified as an asset on the balance sheet of a business firm? 9.____

A. Investment in stock of another firm
B. Premium cost of a three-year fire insurance policy
C. Cash surrender value of life insurance on life of corporate officer. Policy is owned by the company and the company is the beneficiary
D. Amounts owing to employees for services rendered

10. Which one of the following would NOT properly be classified as a current asset? 10.____

A. Travel advances to salespeople
B. Postage in a postage meter
C. Cash surrender value of life insurance policy on an officer, which policy names the corporation as the beneficiary
D. Installment notes receivable due over 18 months in accordance with normal trade practice

11. Able, Baker and Carr formed a partnership. Able contributed $10,000, Baker contributed $5,000, and Carr contributed an automobile with a fair market value of $5,000. They have no partnership agreement. The first year the partnership earned $18,000. The partners will share the profits as follows: 11.____

A. Able, $9,000; Baker, $4,500; Carr, $4,500
B. Able, $6,000; Baker, $6,000; Carr, $6,000
C. Able, $12,000; Baker, $6,000; Carr, No share
D. Able, $8,000; Baker, $5,000; Carr, $5,000

Questions 12-13.

DIRECTIONS: Answer Questions 12 through 13 based on the information below.

The XYZ partnership had the following balance sheet as of December 31, 2018.

Cash	$ 5,000	Liabilities	$ 12,000
Other assets	40,000	X Capital	20,000
Total	$45,000	Y Capital	10,000
		Z Capital	3,000
		Total	$45,000

The partners shared profits equally. They decided to liquidate the partnership at December 31, 2018.

12. If the other assets were sold for $52,000, each partner will be entitled to a final cash distribution of 12.____

A. X, $15,000; Y, $15,000; Z, $15,000
B. X, $24,000; Y, $14,000; Z, $ 7,000
C. X, $20,000; Y, $10,000; Z, $ 3,000
D. X, $23,000; Y, $13,000; Z, $ 6,000

13. If the other assets were sold for $31,000, each partner will be entitled to a final cash distribution of 13.____

A. X, $14,000; Y, $ 5,000; Z, $5,000
B. X, $ 8,000; Y, R 8,000; Z, $8,000
C. X, $15,000; Y, $15,000; Z, $15,000
D. X, $17,000; Y, $ 7,000; Z, No cash share

14. Items selling for $40 for which there were 10% selling costs were purchased for inventory at $20 each. Selling prices and costs remained steady but at the date of the financial statement the market price had dropped to $16. The inventory remaining from the original purchase was written down to $16. 14.____
Of the following, it is correct to state that the

A. cost of sales of the subsequent year will be overstated
B. current year's income is overstated
C. income of the following year will be overstated
D. closing inventory of the current year is overstated

15. Dividends in arrears on a cumulative preferred stock should be reported on the balance sheet as 15.____

A. an accrued liability
B. restricted retained earnings
C. an explanatory note
D. a deduction from preferred stock

16. The effect of recording the payment of a 10% dividend paid in stock would be to 16.____

A. *increase* the current ratio
B. *decrease* the amount of working capital
C. *increase* the total stockholder equity
D. *decrease* the book value per share of stock outstanding

17. The owner of a truck which originally had cost $12,000 but now has a book value of $1,500 was offered $3,000 for it by a used truck dealer. However, the owner traded it in for a new truck listed at $19,000 and received a trade-in allowance of $4,000. The cost basis for the new truck, following the Federal income tax rules, *properly* amounts to 17.____

A. $15,000 B. $16,000 C. $16,500 D. $17,500

18. In planning for purchases to be made during the next month, the following information is to be used: 18.____

Budgeted sales for the month	73,000 units
Inventory at beginning of the month	19,000 units
Planned inventory at end of the month	14,000 units

From the above information, the number of units to be purchased is

A. 40,000 B. 59,000 C. 68,000 D. 78,000

19. A branch office of a company has the following plan: 19.____

Cash balance at beginning of the month	$ 10,000
Planned cash balance at end of the month	$ 15,000
Expected receipts for the month	$ 180,000
Expected disbursements for the month	$ 205,000

In order to comply with this plan, the accountant should recommend that the branch obtain an additional allocation of

A. $20,000 B. $25,000 C. $30,000 D. $50,000

20. A company uses the reserve method of bad debt expense and sets up a Bad Debt account at 2% of sales. The sales were $500,000. The company wrote off $7,500 in accounts receivable. 20.____
The effect of these entries on net income for the period is a(n)

A. $2,500 increase
B. $7,500 decrease
C. $8,000 decrease
D. $10,000 decrease

KEY (CORRECT ANSWERS)

1.	A	11.	B
2.	C	12.	B
3.	B	13.	D
4.	C	14.	C
5.	D	15.	C
6.	C	16.	D
7.	B	17.	C
8.	A	18.	C
9.	D	19.	C
10.	C	20.	D

TEST 2

DIRECTIONS : Each question or incomplete statement is followed by several suggested answers or completions. Select the one that *BEST* answers the question or completes the statement. *PRINT THE LETTER OF THE CORRECT ANSWER IN THE SPACE AT THE RIGHT.*

1. The Delox Corporation has applied to their bank for a $50,000 loan which they will need for 90 days. The bank grants the loan, which will be discounted at 7% interest. The Delox Corporation will receive credit in their account at the bank for (based on a 360-day year): 1.____

   A. $46,500 B. $49,125 C. $50,000 D. $50,875

Questions 2-5.

DIRECTIONS: Answer Questions 2 through 5 based on the information below.

Assume that you are reviewing some accounts of a company and find the following: The Machinery Account and the Accumulated Depreciation - Machinery Account.

MACHINERY

Jan. 1, 2015	Machine #1	20,000	July 1, 2016	6,000
Jan. 1, 2016	Machine #2	16,000		
July 1, 2016	Machine #3	12,000		
Jan. 1, 2018	Machine #4	20,000		

ACCUMULATED DEPRECIATION - MACHINERY

			Dec. 31, 2015	5,000
			Dec. 31, 2016	10,500

Machines are depreciated based upon a four-year life and using the straight-line method. Assume no salvage values.

On July 1, 2016, Machine #1, purchased on January 1, 2015, was sold for $6,000 cash. The bookkeeper debited Cash and credited Machinery for $6,000.

On January 1, 2018, Machine #2 was traded in for a newer model. The new Machine had a list price of $34,000. A trade-in value of $10,000 was granted. $20,000 was paid in cash and the bookkeeper debited Machinery and credited Cash for $20,000. Income-tax rules should have been applied making this entry.

If any errors were made in recording the machine values or depreciation, you are asked to correct them and determine the corrected asset values and proper accumulated depreciation.

2. As of December 31, 2015, you determine that these two accounts 2.____

   A. are correct
   B. are incorrect
   C. overstate asset book values
   D. understate asset book values

3. As of December 31, 2016, you determine that, to correct the Machinery Account Balance, you should leave it 3.____

   A. unchanged B. increased by $6,000
   C. decreased by $14,000 D. decreased by $5,500

4. As of December 31, 2016, you determine that, to reflect the proper balance, the Accumulated Depreciation - Machinery account should 4.____

A. remain unchanged
B. be increased by $10,000
C. be decreased by $10,000
D. be decreased by $ 5,500

5. After the January 1, 2018 entry, you determine that the Machinery Account should, *properly,* 5.____

A. remain unchanged
B. reflect a corrected balance of $52,000
C. reflect a corrected balance of $40,000
D. reflect a corrected balance of $56,000

Questions 6-9.

DIRECTIONS: Answer Questions 6 through 9 based on the information below.

Assume that you are assigned to prepare an Audit Report Summary on the L Company. The L Company uses the accrual method and has an accounting year ending December 31. The bookkeeper of the company has made the following errors:

1. A $1,500 collection from a customer was received on December 29, 2017, but not recorded until the date of its deposit in the bank, January 4, 2018
2. A supplier's $1,900 invoice for inventory items received December 2017 was not recorded until January 2018 (Inventories at December 31, 2017 and 2018 were stated correctly, based on physical count)
3. Depreciation for 2017 was understated by $700
4. In September 2017, a $350 invoice for office supplies was charged to the Utilities Expense account. Office supplies are expensed as purchased
5. December 31, 2017, sales on account of $2,500 were recorded in January 2018, although the merchandise had been shipped and was not in the inventory

Assume that no other errors have occurred and that no correcting entries have been made. Ignore all income taxes.

6. After correcting the errors reported above, the corrected Net Income for 2017 was 6.____

A. overstated by $100
B. understated by $800
C. understated by $1,800
D. neither understated nor overstated

7. Working Capital on December 31, 2017 was 7.____

A. understated by $600
B. understated by $2,300
C. understated by $1,200
D. neither understated nor overstated

8. Total Assets on December 31, 2018 were 8.____

A. overstated by $1,100
B. overstated by $1,800

C. understated by $850
D. neither understated nor overstated

9. The cash balance was 9.____

A. correct as stated originally
B. overstated by $1,500
C. understated by $2,500
D. understated by $1,500

Questions 10-13.

DIRECTIONS: Answer Questions 10 through 13 based on the information below.

Salary expense was listed as a total of $27,600 for the month of June 2018. Withholding taxes were determined to be $7,250 for Income taxes and $1,170 for FICA taxes withheld from employees. Payroll deductions for employee pension fund contribution amounted to $2,500.

Assume the employer's FICA tax share is equal to the employees' and that the employer's share of pension costs is double that of the employees and the employer also pays a 3% Unemployment Insurance Tax based upon $20,000 of the wages paid. The employer pays $1,500 for health insurance plans.

10. The amount of cash that must be obtained to meet this net payroll to pay employees is 10.____

A. $16,680 B. $19,180 C. $20,350 D. $27,600

11. The total payroll tax expense for this payroll period is 11.____

A. $1,170 B. $1,760 C. $2,340 D. $2,940

12. The total liability for withholding and payroll taxes payable is 12.____

A. $2,340 B. $7,250 C. $8,420 D. $10,190

13. The expense of the employer for pension and health-care fringe benefits is 13.____

A. $1,500 B. $2,500 C. $5,000 D. $6,500

14. Currently preferred terminology for statements to be presented limits the use of the term "reserve" to 14.____

A. an actual liability of a known amount
B. estimated liabilities
C. appropriations of retained earnings
D. valuation (contra) accounts

Questions 15-16.

DIRECTIONS: Answer Questions 15 through 16 based on the following.

The Victory Corporation provides an incentive plan whereby its president receives a bonus equal to 10% of the corporate income in excess of $150,000. The bonus is based upon income before income taxes but after calculating the bonus.

15. If the income for the calendar year 2018, before income taxes and before the bonus were $480,000 and the effective tax rate is 40%, the amount of the bonus would be 15.____

A. $15,000 B. $30,000 C. $33,000 D. $48,000

16. The income tax expense for calendar year 2012 would be 16.___

A. $60,000 B. $132,000 C. $180,000 D. $192,000

Questions 17-18.

DIRECTIONS: Answer Questions 17 through 18 based on the information below.

A contract has been awarded to the low bidder. This contractor will then commence construction of a building for the total contract price of $30,000,000. The expected cost of construction is $27,510,000. You are given the additional facts:

	2016	2017	2018
Contract Price as above	$ 30,000,000	$ 30,000,000	$ 30,000,000
Actual Cost to date	$ 9,170,000	$ 13,755,000	$ 27,510,000
Estimated Cost to complete	18,340,000	13,755,000	
Estimated Total Cost	$ 27,510,000	$ 27,510,000	$ 27,510,000
Estimated Total Income	$ 2,490,000	$ ______	$ ______
Billings	$ 9,000,000	$ 9,000,000	$ 9,000,000

17. For 2016, the income to be recognized on a percentage-of-completion basis would be 17.___

A. $830,000
B. $2,490,000
C. $3,000,000
D. $9,000,000

18. For 2017, the income to be recognized by the contractor on a percentage-of-completion basis would be 18.___

A. $415,000 B. $424,500 C. $830,000 D. $1,245,000

19. If the city borrows the $9,000,000 to pay the first billing for the contract above at 10% interest for two years, and the second $9,000,000 at 7% interest for one year, then the interest costs related to this building are, approximately, 19.___

A. $630,000
B. $1,800,000
C. $2,430,000
D. $3,000,000

20. The books of the Monmouth Corporation show the following: 20.___

	2018	2017	2016
Average earnings for prior 3 years	$70,000	$75,000	$78,000
Net tangible assets	$40,000	$42,000	$50,000

If it is expected that 15% would be normal earnings on net tangible assets, then the *average* excess earnings are

A. $7,120 B. $8,333 C. $9,800 D. $10,800

21. A business showed the following figures in its accounts for the year 2018: 21.___

Sales - $346,000
Inventory, December 31, 2018 - $58,000
Inventory, December 31, 2017 - $52,000
Purchases - $274,000
Operating Expenses - $36,000

The gross profit earned by this concern is

A. $72,000 B. $42,000 C. $66,000 D. $78,000

22. A business firm buys an article for $320, less 40% and 10%, terms 2/10 n/30, on March 18. If it pays the bill on March 27, it should pay 22.____

A. $169.34 B. $172.80 C. $160.00 D. $156.80

23. In the partnership of Danvers and Edwards, Danvers has a capital of $10,000 and Edwards has a capital of $15,000. If Furgal wishes to invest $11,000 and thereby receive a 1/4 interest in the business, the goodwill in the business has been computed to be worth 23.____

A. $19,000 B. $33,000 C. $14,000 D. $8,000

24. George Bailey's capital at the beginning of the year was $14,000. At the end of the year his assets were $62,000 and his liabilities were $39,000. His drawings for the year amounted to $6,000.
His profit for the year was 24.____

A. $15,000 B. $3,000 C. $9,000 D. $17,000

25. George Wilson's check book shows the following: 25.____

Balance at the beginning of the month	-$3,517.42
Deposits during the month	-$1,923.98
Checks drawn during the month	-$2,144.36

In going over his bank statement, he finds that a deposit of $455.64 made by him has not yet been credited by the bank and that the bank has charged him $9.40 for services rendered. He also finds that he has outstanding checks totaling $268.19.
His bank statement balance should be printed as

A. $3,100.19 B. $3,118.99 C. $2,563.81 D. $4,011.47

KEY (CORRECT ANSWERS)

1. B
2. A
3. C
4. C
5. C

6. A
7. A
8. B
9. D
10. A

11. B
12. D
13. D
14. C
15. B

16. C
17. A
18. A
19. C
20. B

21. D
22. A
23. D
24. A
25. A

ACCOUNTING

EXAMINATION SECTION

TEST 1

DIRECTIONS: Each question or incomplete statement is followed by several suggested answers or completions. Select the one that BEST answers the question or completes the statement. *PRINT THE LETTER OF THE CORRECT ANSWER IN THE SPACE AT THE RIGHT.*

Questions 1-5.

DIRECTIONS: Questions 1 through 5 are to be answered on the basis of the following information.

When balance sheets are analyzed, working capital always receives close attention. Adequate working capital enables a company to carry sufficient inventories, meet current debts, take advantage of cash discounts and extend favorable terms to customers. A company that is deficient in working capital and unable to do these things is in a poor competitive position.

Below is a Trial Balance as of June 30, 2021, in alphabetical order, of the Worth Corporation.

	Debits	Credits
Accounts Payable		$50,000
Accounts Receivable	$40,000	
Accrued Expenses Payable		10,000
Capital Stock		10,000
Cash	20,000	
Depreciation Expense	5,000	
Inventory	60,000	
Plant & Equipment (net)	30,000	
Retained Earnings		20,000
Salary Expense	35,000	
Sales		100,000
	$190,000	$190,000

1. The Worth Corporation's Working Capital, based on the data above, is 1.____
   A. $50,000 B. $55,000 C. $60,000 D. $65,000

2. Which one of the following transactions increases Working Capital? 2.____
   A. Collecting outstanding accounts receivable
   B. Borrowing money from the bank based upon a 90-day interest-bearing note payable
   C. Paying off a 60-day note payable to the bank
   D. Selling merchandise at a profit

3. The Worth Corporation's Current Ratio, based on the above data, is 3.____
   A. 1.7 to 1 B. 2 to 1 C. 2.5 to 1 D. 4 to 3

4. Which one of the following transactions decreases the Current Ratio? 4.____
   A. Collecting an account receivable
   B. Borrowing money from the bank giving a 90-day interest-bearing note payable
   C. Paying off a 60-day note payable to the bank
   D. Selling merchandise at a profit

5. The payment of a current liability, such as Payroll Taxes Payable, will 5.____
   A. *increase* the current ratio but have no effect on the working capital
   B. *increase* the Working Capital, but have no effect on the current ratio
   C. *decrease* both the current ratio and working capital
   D. *increase* both the current ratio and working capital

6. During the year 2021, the Ramp Equipment Co. made sales to customers totaling $100,000 that were subject to sales taxes of $8,000. Net cash collections totaled $92,000. Discounts of $3,000 were allowed. During the year 2021, uncollectible accounts in the sum of $2,000 were written off the books. 6.____
   The net change in accounts receivable during the year 2021 was
   A. $10,500 B. $11,000 C. $13,000 D. $13,500

7. The Grable Co. received a $6,000, 8%, 60-day note dated May 1, 2021 from a customer. On May 16, 2021, the Grable Co. discounted the note at 6% at the bank. 7.____
   The net proceeds from the discounting of the note amounted to
   A. $5,954.40 B. $6,034.40 C. $6,064.80 D. $6,080.00

8. In reviewing the customers' accounts in the Accounts Receivable Ledger for the entire year 2020, the following errors are discovered. 8.____
   - A sale in the amount of $500 to the J. Brown Co. was erroneously posted to the K. Brown Co.
   - A sales return of $100 from the Gale Co. was debited to their account.
   - A check was received from a customer, M. White and Co. in payment of a sale of $500 less 2% discount. The check was entered properly in the cash receipts book but was posted to the M. White and Co. account in the amount of $490.

   The difference between the controlling account and its related accounts receivable schedule amounts to
   A. $90 B. $110 C. $190 D. $210

9. Assume that you are called upon to audit a cash fund. You find in the cash drawer postage stamps and I.O.U.'s signed by employees, totaling together $425. 9.____
   In preparing a financial report, the $425 should be reported as
   A. petty cash B. investments
   C. supplies and receivables D. cash

10. On December 31, 2020, before adjustment, Accounts Receivable had a debit balance of $60,000 and the Allowance for Uncollectible Accounts had a debit balance of $1,000. 10.____
If credit losses are estimated at 5% of Accounts Receivable and the estimated method of reporting bad debts is used, then bad debts expense for the year 2020 would be reported as
A. $1,000 B. $2,000 C. $3,000 D. $4,000

Questions 11-12.

DIRECTIONS: Questions 11 and 12 are to be answered on the basis of the following information.

Accrued salaries payable on $7,500 had not been recorded on December 31, 2021. Office supplies on hand of $2,500 at December 32, 2021 were erroneously treated as expense instead of inventory. Neither of these errors was discovered or corrected.

11. These two errors would cause the income for 4021 to be 11.____
A. *understated* by $5,000 B. *overstated* by $5,000
C. *understated* by $10,000 D. *overstated* by $10,000

12. The effect of these errors on the retained earnings at December 31, 2021 would be 12.____
A. *understated* by $2,500 B. *overstated* by $2,500
C. *understated* by $5,000 D. *overstated* by $5,000

Questions 13-14.

DIRECTIONS: Questions 13 and 14 are to be answered on the basis of the following information.

Albano, Borrone, and Colluci operate a retail store under the trade name of ABC. Their partnership agreement provides for equaling sharing profits and losses after salaries of $5,000 to Albano, $10,000 to Borrone, and $15,000 to Colluci.

13. If the net income of the partnership (prior to salaries to partners) is $21,000, then Albano's share of the profits, considering all aspects of the agreement, is determined to be 13.____
A. $2,000 B. $3,000 C. $5,000 D. $7,000

14. The share of the profits that apply to Borrone, similarly, is determined to be 14.____
A. $2,000 B. $3,000 C. $5,000 D. $7,000

Questions 15-17.

DIRECTIONS: Questions 15 through 17 are to be answered on the basis of the following information.

The Kay Company currently uses FIFO for inventory valuation. Their records for the year ended June 30, 2021 reflect the following:

July 1, 2021 inventory	100,000 units @ 7.50
Purchases during year	400,000 units @ $8.00
Sales during year	350,000 units @ $15.00
Expenses exclusive of income taxes	$1,290,000
Cash balance on June 30, 2021	$250,000
Income tax rate	34%

Assume the July 1, 2021 inventory will be the LIFO Base Inventory.

15. If the company should change to the LIFO as of June 30, 2021, then their income before taxes for the year-ended June 30, 2021, as compared with the income FIFO method, will be 15.____
    A. *increased* by $50,000
    B. *decreased* by $50,000
    C. *increased* by $100,000
    D. *decreased* by $100,000

16. Assuming the given tax rate (45%), the use of the LIFO method will result in an approximate tax expense for fiscal 2021 of 16.____
    A. $45,000 B. $50,000 C. $72,000 D. $94,500

17. Assuming the given tax rate (45%), the use of the LIFO inventory method compared with the FIFO method, will result in a change in the approximate income tax expense for fiscal year 2021 as follows: 17.____
    A. *Increase* of $22,500
    B. *Decrease* of $22,500
    C. *Increase* of $45,000
    D. *Decrease* of $45,000

18. An accountant in an agency, in addition to his regular duties, has been assigned to train a newly appointed assistant accountant. The latter believes that he is not being given the training that he needs in order to perform his duties. Accordingly, the MOST appropriate FIRST step for the assistant accountant to take in order to secure the needed training is to 18.____
    A. register for the appropriate courses at the local college as soon as possible
    B. advise the accountant in a formal memo that his apparent lack of interest in the training is impeding his progress
    C. discuss the matter with the accountant privately and try to discover what seems to be the problem
    D. secure such training informally from more sympathetic accountants in the agency

19. You have worked very hard and successfully helped complete a difficult audit of a large corporation doing business with your agency. Your supervisor gives you a brief nod of approval when you expected a more substantial degree of recognition. You are angry and feel unappreciated. 19.____

Of the following, the MOST appropriate course of action for you to take would be to

A. voice your displeasure to your fellow workers at being taken for granted by an unappreciative supervisor
B. say nothing now and assume that your supervisor's nod of approval may be his customary acknowledgment of efforts well done
C. let your supervisor know that he owes you something by repeatedly stressing the outstanding job you've done
D. ease off on your work quality and productivity until your efforts are finally appreciated

20. You have been assisting in an audit of the books and records of businesses as a member of a team. The accountant in charge of your group tells you to start preliminary work independently on a new audit. This audit is to take place at the offices of the business. The business officers have been duly notified of the audit date. Upon arrival at their offices, you find that their records and files are in disarray and that their personnel are antagonistic and uncooperative. 20.____

Of the following, the MOST desirable action for you to take is to

A. advise the business officers that serious consequences may follow unless immediate cooperation is secured
B. accept whatever may be shown or told you on the grounds that it would be unwise to further antagonize uncooperative personnel
C. inform your supervisor of the situation and request instructions
D. leave immediately and return later in the expectation of encountering a more cooperative attitude

KEY (CORRECT ANSWERS)

1.	C	11.	C
2.	D	12.	A
3.	B	13.	A
4.	B	14.	D
5.	A	15.	B
6.	B	16.	C
7.	B	17.	B
8.	D	18.	C
9.	C	19.	B
10.	D	20.	C

TEST 2

DIRECTIONS: Each question or incomplete statement is followed by several suggested answers or completions. Select the one that BEST answers the question or completes the statement. *PRINT THE LETTER OF THE CORRECT ANSWER IN THE SPACE AT THE RIGHT.*

Questions 1-3.

DIRECTIONS: Questions 1 through 3 are to be answered on the basis of the following information.

The city is planning to borrow money with a 5-year, 7% bond issue totaling $10,000,000 on principle when other municipal issues are paying 8%.

Present value of $1 – 8% - 5 years -68057

Present value of annual interest payments – annuity 8% - 5 years – 3.99271

1. The funds obtained from this bond issue (ignoring any costs relating to issuance) would be, approximately, 1.____
   A. $9,515,390 B. $10,000,000 C. $10,484,620 D. $10,800,000

2. At the date of maturity, the bonds will be redeemed at 2.____
   A. $9,515,390 B. $10,000,000 C. $10,484,610 D. $10,800,000

3. As a result of this issue, the ACTUAL interest costs each year as related to the 7% interest payments will 3.____
   A. be the same as paid ($700,000)
   B. be more than $700,000
   C. be less than $700,000
   D. fluctuate depending on the market conditions

4. Following the usual governmental accounting concepts, the activities of a municipal employee retirement plan, which is financed by equal employer and employee contributions, should be accounted for in a(n) 4.____
   A. agency fund
   B. intragovernmental service fund
   C. special assessment fund
   D. trust fund

Questions 5-7.

DIRECTIONS: Questions 5 through 7 are to be answered on the basis of the following information.

The Balance Sheet of the JLA Corp. is as follows:

Current Assets	$50,000	Current Liabilities	$20,000
Other Assets	75,000	Common Stock	75,000
Total	$125,000	Retained Earnings	30,000
		Total	$125,000

5. The working capital of the JLA Corp. is 5.____
   A. $30,000 B. $50,000 C. $105,000 D. $125,000

6. The operating ratio of the JLA Corp. is 6.____
   A. 2 to 1 B. 2½ to 1 C. 1 to 2 D. 1 to 2½

7. The stockholders' equity is 7.____
   A. $30,000 B. $75,000 C. $105,000 D. $125,000

8. This question is based on the following figures taken from a set of books for the year ending June 30, 2021. 8.____

	Trial Balance Before Adjustments	Trial Balance After Adjustments
Commissions Payable	cr...	cr $1,550
Office Salaries	dr $9,500	dr $10,680
Rental Income	cr $4,300	cr $4,900
Accumulated Depreciation	cr $7,000	cr $9,700
Supplies Expense	dr $1,760	dr $1,200

As a result of the adjustments reflected in the adjusted trial balance, the net income of the company before taxes will be
   A. *increased* by $4,270 B. *decreased* by $4,270
   C. *increased* by $5,430 D. *decreased* by $5,430

9. This question is based on the following facts concerning the operations of a manufacturer of office desks. 9.____

Jan. 1, 2021	Goods in Process Inventory	4,260 units	40% complete
Dec. 31, 2021	Goods in Process Inventory	3,776 units	25% complete
Jan. 1, 2021	Finished Goods Inventory	2,630 units	
Dec. 31, 2021	Finished Goods Inventory	3,180 units	

Sales consummated during the year: 127,460 units

Assuming that all the desks are the same style, the number of equivalent complete units, manufactured during the year 2021 is
   A. 127,250 B. 127,460 C. 128,010 D. 131,510

Questions 10-11.

DIRECTIONS: Questions 10 and 11 are to be answered on the basis of the following information.

On January 1, 2021, the Lenox Corporation was organized with a cash investment of $50,000 by the shareholders. Some of the corporate records were destroyed. However, you were able to discover the following facts from various sources.

Accounts Payable at December 31, 2021 (arising from merchandise purchased)	$16,000
Accounts Receivable at December 31, 2021 (arising from the sales of merchandise)	$18,000
Sales for the calendar year 2021	$94,000
Inventory, December 31, 2021	20,000
Cost of Goods Sold is 60% of the selling price	
Bank loan outstanding – December 31, 2021	15,000
Expenses paid in cash during the year	35,000
Expenses incurred but unpaid as of December 31, 2021	4,000
Dividend paid	25,000

10. The CORRECT cash balance is 10.____
 A. $5,600 B. $20,600 C. $38,600 D. $40,600

11. The stockholders' equity on December 31, 2021 is 11.____
 A. $23,600 B. Deficit of $26,400
 C. $27,600 D. $42,400

Questions 12-13.

DIRECTIONS: Questions 12 and 13 are to be answered on the basis of the following facts developed from the records of a company that sells its merchandise on the installment plan.

Sales	Calendar Year 2020	Calendar Year 2021
Total volume of sales	$80,000	$100,000
Cost of Goods Sold	60,000	40,000
Gross Profit	$20,000	$60,000
Cash Collections		
From 2020 Sales	$18,000	$36,000
From 2021 Sales		22,000
Total Cash Collections	$18,000	$58,000

12. Using the deferred profit method of determining thee income from installment sales, the gross profit on sales for the calendar year 2020 was 12.____
 A. $4,500 B. $18,000 C. $20,000 D. None

13. Using the deferred profit method of determining the income from installment sales, the gross profit on sales for the calendar year 2021 was 13.____
 A. $22,000 B. $22,200 C. $60,000 D. None

Questions 14-15.

DIRECTIONS: Questions 14 and 15 are to be answered on the basis of the data developed from an examination of the records of Ralston, Inc. for the month of April 2021.

Beginning Inventory: 10,000 units @ $4.00 each

	Purchases		Sales
April 10	20,000 units @ $5 each	April 13	15,000 units @ $8 each
17	60,000 units @ $6 each	21	50,000 units @ $9 each
26	40,000 units @ $7 each	27	50,000 units @ $10 each

14. The gross profit on sales for the month of April, 2021, assuming that inventory is priced on the FIFO basis, is 14.____
    A. $330,000 B. $355,000 C. $395,000 D. $435,000

15. The gross profit on sales for the month of April 2021, assuming that inventory is priced on the LIFO basis is 15.____
    A. $330,000 B. $355,000 C. $395,000 D. $435,000

16. This question is to be answered on the basis of the data presented for June 30, 2021. 16.____

Balance per Bank Statement	$24,019.00
Balance per General Ledger	20,592.64
Proceeds of note collected by the bank which had not been recorded in the Cash account	4,000.00
Interest on note collected by the bank (no book entries made0	39.40
Debit memo for Bank charges for the month of May	23.50
Deposit in Transit (June 30, 2021)	2,144.00
Customer's check returned by the bank due to lack of funds	150.00
Outstanding checks – June 30, 2021	1,631.46
Error in recording check made by our bookkeeper – check cleared in the amount of $463.00 but entered in the bank book for $436.00	

If we wish to reconcile the bank and book balance so that the bank balance and the book balance are reconciled to a corrected balance, the corrected balance should be
    A. $20,592.64 B. $24,019.00 C. $24,531.54 D. $26,163.00

17. The Ateb Company has issued a $500,000 bond issue on January 2, 2021 at 8% interest, payable semi-annually, sold at par, with interest payable on June 30 and December 31. 17.____
    On September 30, 2021, at the close of the fiscal year of the Ateb Company, the interest expense accrual should reflect interest payable of, approximately,
    A. $10,000 B. $20,000 C. $40,000 D. $50,000

18. Assume that a new procedure requires that a particular and unvarying sequence of steps be followed in order to yield the desired data. You are assigned to be in charge of subordinates working with this procedure. 18.____

Which one of the following is MOST likely to impress subordinates with the importance of following the sequence of steps exactly as given?
A. Explain the consequences of error if the procedure is not followed.
B. Suggest how rewarding would be the feeling of finding errors before the supervisor catches them.
C. Indicate that independent verification of their work will be done by other staff members
D. Advise that upward career mobility usually results from following instructions exactly

19. It is essential for an experienced accountant to know approximately how long it will take him to complete a particular assignment because 19.____
A. his supervisors will need to obtain this information only from someone planning to perform the assignment
B. he must arrange his schedule to insure proper completion of the assignment consistent with agency objectives
C. he must measure whether he is keeping pace with others performing similar assignments
D. he must determine what assignments are essential and have the greatest priority within his agency

20. There are circumstances which call for special and emergency efforts by employees. You must assign your staff to make this type of effort. 20.____
Of the following, this special type of assignment is MOST likely to succeed if the
A. time schedule required to complete the assignment is precisely stated but is not adhered to
B. employees are individually free to determine the work schedule
C. assignment is clearly defined
D. employees are individually free to use any procedure or method available to them

KEY (CORRECT ANSWERS)

1.	A	11.	A
2.	B	12.	A
3.	B	13.	B
4.	D	14.	C
5.	A	15.	B
6.	B	16.	C
7.	C	17.	A
8.	B	18.	A
9.	A	19.	B
10.	B	20.	C

READING COMPREHENSION
UNDERSTANDING AND INTERPRETING WRITTEN MATERIAL

EXAMINATION SECTION

TEST 1

DIRECTIONS: Each question or incomplete statement is followed by several suggested answers or completions. Select the one that BEST answers the question or completes the statement. *PRINT THE LETTER OF THE CORRECT ANSWER IN THE SPACE AT THE RIGHT.*

Questions 1-5.

DIRECTIONS: Questions 1 through 5 are to be answered SOLELY on the basis of the following passage.

The most effective control mechanism to prevent gross incompetence on the part of public employees is a good personnel program. The personnel officer in the line departments and the central personnel agency should exert positive leadership to raise levels of performance. Although the key factor is the quality of the personnel recruited, staff members other than personnel officers can make important contributions to efficiency. Administrative analysts, now employed in many agencies, make detailed studies of organization and procedures, with the purpose of eliminating delays, waste, and other inefficiencies. Efficiency is, however, more than a question of good organization and procedures; it is also the product of the attitudes and value of the public employees. Personal motivation can provide the will to be efficient. The best management studies will not result in substantial improvement of the performance of those employees who feel no great urge to wok up to their abilities.

1. The above passage indicates that the KEY factor in preventing gross incompetence of public employees is the — 1.____
   - A. hiring of administrative analysts to assist personnel people
   - B. utilization of effective management studies
   - C. overlapping of responsibility
   - D. quality of the employees hired

2. According to the above passage, the central personnel agency staff SHOULD — 2.____
   - A. work more closely with administrative analysts in the line departments than with personnel officers
   - B. make a serious effort to avoid jurisdictional conflicts with personnel officers in line departments
   - C. contribute to improving the quality of work of public employees
   - D. engage in a comprehensive program to change the public's negative image of public employees

3. The above passage indicates that efficiency in an organization can BEST be brought about by 3.____
   A. eliminating ineffective control mechanisms
   B. instituting sound organizational procedures
   C. promoting competent personnel
   D. recruiting people with desire to do good work

4. According to the above passage, the purpose of administrative analysts in a public agency is to 4.____
   A. prevent injustice to the public employee
   B. promote the efficiency of the agency
   C. protect the interests of the public
   D. ensure the observance of procedural due process

5. The above passage implies that a considerable rise in the quality of work of public employees can be brought about by 5.____
   A. encouraging positive employee attitudes toward work
   B. controlling personnel officers who exceed their powers
   C. creating warm personal associations among public employees in an agency
   D. closing loopholes in personnel organization and procedures

Questions 6-8.

DIRECTIONS: Questions 6 through 8 are to be answered SOLELY on the basis of the following passage.

<u>EMPLOYEE NEEDS</u>

The greatest waste in industry and in government may be that of human resources. This waste usually derives not from employees' unwillingness or inability, but from management's ineptness to meet the maintenance and motivational needs of employees. Maintenance needs refer to such needs as providing employees with safe places to work, written work rules, job security, adequate salary, employer-sponsored social activities, and with knowledge of their role in the overall framework of the organization. However, of greatest significance to employees are the motivational needs of job growth, achievement, responsibility, and recognition.

Although employee dissatisfaction may stem from either poor maintenance or poor motivation factors, the outward manifestation of the dissatisfaction may be very much like, i.e., negativism, complaints, deterioration of performance, and so forth. The improvement in the lighting of an employee's work area or raising his level of ay won't do much good if the source of the dissatisfaction is the absence of a meaningful assignment. By the same token, if an employee is dissatisfied with what he considers inequitable pay, the introduction of additional challenge in his work may simply make matters worse.

It is relatively easy for an employee to express frustration by complaining about pay, washroom conditions, fringe benefits, and so forth; but most people cannot easily express resentment in terms of the more abstract concepts concerning job growth, responsibility, and achievement.

It would be wrong to assume that there is no interaction between maintenance and motivational needs of employee. For example, conditions of high motivation often overshadow poor maintenance conditions. If an organization is in a period of strong growth and expansion, opportunities for job growth, responsibility, recognition, and achievement are usually abundant, but the rapid growth may have outrun the upkeep of maintenance factors. In this situation, motivation may be high, but only if employees recognize the poor maintenance conditions as unavoidable and temporary. The subordination of maintenance factors cannot go on indefinitely, even with the highest motivation.

Both maintenance and motivation factors influence the behavior of all employees, but employees are not identical and, furthermore, the needs of any individual do not remain orientation toward maintenance factors and those with greater sensitivity toward motivation factors.

A highly maintenance-oriented individual, preoccupied with the factors peripheral to his job rather than the job itself, is more concerned with comfort than challenge. He does not get deeply involved with his work but does with the condition of his work area, toilet facilities, and his time for going to lunch. By contrast, a strongly motivation-oriented employee is usually relatively indifferent to his surroundings and is caught up in the pursuit of work goals.

Fortunately, there are few people who are either exclusively maintenance-oriented or purely motivation-oriented. The former would be deadwood in an organization, while the latter might trample on those around him in his pursuit to achieve his goals.

6. With respect to employee motivational and maintenance needs, the management policies of an organization which is growing rapidly will probably result 6.____
   A. more in meeting motivational needs rather than maintenance needs
   B. more in meeting maintenance needs rather than motivational needs
   C. in meeting both of these needs equally
   D. in increased effort to define the motivational and maintenance needs of its employees

7. In accordance with the above passage, which of the following CANNOT be considered as an example of an employee maintenance need for railroad clerks? 7.____
   A. Providing more relief periods
   B. Providing fair salary increases at periodic intervals
   C. Increasing job responsibilities
   D. Increasing health insurance benefits

8. Most employees in an organization may be categorized as being interested in 8.____
   A. maintenance needs only
   B. motivational needs only
   C. both motivational and maintenance needs
   D. money only, to the exclusion of all other needs

Questions 9-11.

DIRECTIONS: Questions 9 through 11 are to be answered SOLELY on the basis of the following passage.

GOOD EMPLOYEE PRACTICES

As a city employee, you will be expected to take an interest in you work and perform the duties of your job to the best of your ability and in a spirit of cooperation. Nothing shows an interest in your work more than coming to work on time, not only at the start of the day but also when returning from lunch. If it is necessary for you to keep a personal appointment at lunch hour which might cause a delay in getting back to work on time, you should explain the situation to your supervisor and get his approval to come back a little late before you leave for lunch.

You should do everything that is asked of you willingly and consider important even the small jobs that your supervisor gives you. Although these jobs may seem unimportant, if you forget to do them or if you don't do them right, trouble may develop later.

Getting along well with your fellow workers will add much to the enjoyment of your work. You should respect your fellow workers and try to see their side when a disagreement arises. The better you get along with your fellow workers and your supervisor, the better you will like your job and the better you will be able to do it.

9. According to the above passage, in your job as a city employee, you are expected to 9.____
   A. show a willingness to cooperate on the job
   B. get your supervisor's approval before keeping any personal appointments at lunch hour
   C. avoid doing small jobs that seem unimportant
   D. do the easier jobs at the start of the day and the more difficult ones later on

10. According to the above passage, getting to work on time shows that you 10.____
   A. need the job
   B. have an interest in your work
   C. get along well with your fellow workers
   D. like your supervisor

11. According to the above passage, the one of the following statements that is NOT true is: 11.____
   A. If you do a small job wrong, trouble may develop
   B. You should respect your fellow workers
   C. If you disagree with a fellow worker, you should try to see his side of the story
   D. The less you get along with your supervisor, the better you will be able to do your job

Questions 12-15.

DIRECTIONS: Questions 12 through 15 are to be answered SOLELY on the basis of the following passage.

EMPLOYEE SUGGESTIONS

To increase the effectiveness of the city government, the city asks its employees to offer suggestions when they feel an improvement could be made in some government operation. The Employees' Suggestions Program was started to encourage city employees to do this. Through this Program, which is only for city employees, cash awards may be given to those whose suggestions are submitted and approved. Suggestions are looked for not only from supervisors but from all city employees as any city employee may get an idea which might be approved and contribute greatly to the solution of some problem of city government.

Therefore, all suggestions for improvement are welcome, whether they be suggestions on how to improve working conditions, or on how to increase the speed with which work is done, or on how to reduce or eliminate such things as waste, time losses, accidents or fire hazards. There are, however, a few types of suggestions for which cash awards cannot be given. An example of this type would be a suggestion to increase salaries or a suggestion to change the regulations about annual leave or about sick leave. The number of suggestions sent in has increased sharply during the past few years. It is hoped that it will keep increasing in the future in order to meet the city's needs for more ideas for improved ways of doing things.

12. According to the above passage, the MAIN reason why the city asks its employees for suggestions about government operations is to 12.____
   A. increase the effectiveness of the city government
   B. show that the Employees' Suggestion Program is working well
   C. show that everybody helps run the city government
   D. have the employee win a prize

13. According to the above passage, the Employees' Suggestion Program can approve awards ONLY for those suggestions that come from 13.____
   A. city employees
   B. city employees who are supervisors
   C. city employees who are not supervisors
   D. experienced employee of the city

14. According to the above passage, a cash award cannot be given through the Employees' Suggestion Program for a suggestion about 14.____
   A. getting work done faster
   B. helping prevent accidents on the job
   C. increasing the amount of annual leave for city employees
   D. reducing the chance of fire where city employees work

15. According to the above passage, the suggestions sent in during the past few years have 15.____
    A. all been approved
    B. generally been well written
    C. been mostly about reducing or eliminating waste
    D. been greater in number than before

Questions 16-18.

DIRECTIONS: Questions 16 through 18 are to be answered SOLELY on the basis of the following passage.

The supervisor will gain the respect of the members of his staff and increase his influence over them by controlling his temper and avoiding criticizing anyone publicly. When a mistake is made, the good supervisor will take it over with the employee quietly and privately. The supervisor will listen to the employee's story, suggest the better way of doing the job, and offer help so the mistake won't happen again. Before closing the discussion, the supervisor should try to find something good to say about other parts of the employee's work. Some praise and appreciation, along with instruction, is more likely to encourage an employee to improve in those areas where he is weakest.

16. A good title that would show the meaning of the above passage would be 16.____
    A. How to Correct Employee Errors
    B. How to Praise Employees
    C. Mistakes are Preventable
    D. The Weak Employee

17. According to the above passage, the work of an employee who has made a mistake is more likely to improve if the supervisor 17.____
    A. avoids criticizing him
    B. gives him a chance to suggest a better way of doing the work
    C. listens to the employee's excuses to see if he is right
    D. praises good work at the same time he corrects the mistake

18. According to the above passage, when a supervisor needs to correct an employee's mistake, it is important that he 18.____
    A. allow some time to go by after the mistake is made
    B. do so when other employee are not present
    C. show his influence with his tone of voice
    D. tell other employee to avoid the same mistake

Questions 19-23.

DIRECTIONS: Questions 19 through 23 are to be answered SOLELY on the basis of the following passage.

In studying the relationships of people to the organizational structure, it is absolutely necessary to identify and recognize the informal organizational structure. These relationships are necessary when coordination of a plan is attempted. They may be with *the boss*, line supervisors, staff personnel, or other representatives of the formal organization's hierarchy, and they may include the *liaison men* who serve as the leaders of the informal organization. An acquaintanceship with the people serving in these roles in the organization, and its formal counterpart, permits a supervisor to recognize sensitive areas in which it is simple to get conflict reaction. Avoidance of such areas, plus conscious efforts to inform other people of his own objectives for various plans, will usually enlist their aid and support. Planning *without* people can lead to disaster because the individuals who must act together to make any plan a success are more important than the plans themselves.

19. Of the following titles, the one that MOST clearly describes the above passage is 19.____
    A. Coordination of a Function
    B. Avoidance of Conflict
    C. Planning With People
    D. Planning Objectives

20. According to the above passage, attempts at coordinating plans may fail unless 20.____
    A. the plan's objectives are clearly set forth
    B. conflict between groups is resolved
    C. the plans themselves are worthwhile
    D. informal relationships are recognized

21. According to the above passage, conflict 21.____
    A. may, in some cases, be desirable to secure results
    B. produces more heat than light
    C. should be avoided at all costs
    D. possibilities can be predicted by a sensitive supervisor

22. The above passage implies that 22.____
    A. informal relationships are more important than formal structure
    B. the weakness of a formal structure depends upon informal relationships
    C. liaison men are the key people to consult when taking formal and informal structures into account
    D. individuals in a group are at least as important as the plans for the group

23. The above passage suggests that 23.____
    A. some planning can be disastrous
    B. certain people in sensitive areas should be avoided
    C. the supervisor should discourage acquaintanceships in the organization
    D. organizational relationships should be consciously limited

Questions 24-25.

DIRECTIONS: Questions 24 and 25 are to be answered SOLELY on the basis of the following passage.

Good personnel relations of an organization depend upon mutual confidence, trust, and good will. The basis of confidence is understanding. Most troubles start with people who do not understand each other. When the organization's intentions or motives are misunderstood, or when reasons for actions, practices, or policies are misconstrued, complete cooperation from individuals is not forthcoming. If management expects full cooperation from employees, it has a responsibility of sharing with them the information which is the foundation of proper understanding, confidence, and trust. Personnel management has long since outgrown the days when it was the vogue to *treat them rough and tell them nothing.* Up-to-date personnel management provides all possible information about the activities, aims, and purposes of the organization. It seems altogether creditable that a desire should exist among employees for such information which the best-intentioned executive might think would not interest them and which the worst-intentioned would think was none of their business.

24. The above passage implies that one of the causes of the difficulty which an organization might have with its personnel relations is that its employees 24.____
    A. have not expressed interest in the activities, aims, and purposes of the organization
    B. do not believe in the good faith of the organization
    C. have not been able to give full cooperation to the organization
    D. do not recommend improvements in the practices and policies of the organization

25. According to the above passage, in order for an organization to have good personnel relations, it is NOT essential that 25.____
    A. employees have confidence in the organization
    B. the purposes of the organization be understood by the employees
    C. employees have a desire for information about the organization
    D. information about the organization be communicated to employees

---

KEY (CORRECT ANSWERS)

1.	D	11.	D
2.	C	12.	A
3.	D	13.	A
4.	B	14.	C
5.	A	15.	D
6.	A	16.	A
7.	C	17.	D
8.	C	18.	B
9.	A	19.	C
10.	B	20.	D

21.	D
22.	D
23.	A
24.	B
25.	C

TEST 2

DIRECTIONS: Each question or incomplete statement is followed by several suggested answers or completions. Select the one that BEST answers the question or completes the statement. *PRINT THE LETTER OF THE CORRECT ANSWER IN THE SPACE AT THE RIGHT.*

Questions 1-8.

DIRECTIONS: Questions 1 through 8 are to be answered SOLELY on the basis of the following passage.

Important figures in education and in public affairs have recommended development of a private organization sponsored in part by various private foundations which would offer installment payment plans to full-time matriculated students in accredited colleges and universities in the United States and Canada. Contracts would be drawn to cover either tuition and fees, or tuition, fees, room and board in college facilities, from one year up to and including six years. A special charge, which would vary with the length of the contract, would be added to the gross repayable amount. This would be in addition to interest at a rate which would vary with the income of the parents. There would be a 3% annual interest charge for families with total income, before income taxes, of $50,000 or less. The rate would increase by 1/10 of 1% for every $1,000 of additional net income in excess of $50,000 up to a maximum of 10% interest. Contracts would carry an insurance provision on the life of the parent or guardian who signs the contract; all contracts must have the signature of a parent or guardian. Payment would be scheduled in equal monthly installments.

1. Which of the following students would be eligible for the payment plan described in the above passage? A 1.____
   - A. matriculated student taking six semester hours toward a graduate degree
   - B. matriculated student taking seventeen semester hours toward an undergraduate degree
   - C. graduate matriculated at the University of Mexico taking eighteen semester hours toward a graduate degree
   - D. student taking eighteen semester hours in a special pre-matriculation program

2. According to the above passage, the organization described would be sponsored in part by 2.____
   - A. private foundations
   - B. colleges and universities
   - C. persons in the field of education
   - D. persons in public life

3. Which of the following expenses could NOT be covered by a contract with the organization described in the above passage? 3.____
   - A. Tuition amounting to $20,000 per year
   - B. Registration and laboratory fees
   - C. Meals at restaurants near the college
   - D. Rent for an apartment in a college dormitory

4. The total amount to be paid would include ONLY the 4.____
   A. principal
   B. principal and interest
   C. principal, interest, and special charge
   D. principal, interest, special charge, and fee

5. The contract would carry insurance on the 5.____
   A. life of the student
   B. life of the student's parents
   C. income of the parents of the student
   D. life of the parent who signed the contract

6. The interest rate for an annual loan of $25,000 from the organization described in the above passage for a student whose family's net income was $55,000 should be 6.____
   A. 3% B. 3.5% C. 4% D. 4.5%

7. The interest rate for an annual loan of $35,000 from the organization described in the above passage for a student whose family's net income was $100,000 should be 7.____
   A. 5% B. 8% C. 9% D. 10%

8. John Lee has submitted an application for the installment payment plan described in the above passage. John's mother and father have a store which grossed $500,000 last year, but the income which the family received from the store was $90,000 before taxes. They also had $5,000 income from stock dividends. They paid $10,000 in income taxes. 8.____
   The amount of income upon which the interest should be based is
   A. $85,000 B. $90,000 C. $95,000 D. $105,000

Questions 9-13.

DIRECTIONS: Questions 9 through 13 are to be answered SOLELY on the basis of the following passage.

Since the organization chart is pictorial in nature, there is a tendency for it to be drawn in an artistically balanced and appealing fashion, regardless of the realities of actual organizational structure. In addition to being subject to this distortion, there is the difficulty of communicating in any organization chart the relative importance or the relative size of various component parts of an organizational structure. Furthermore, because of the need for simplicity of design, an organization chart can never indicate the full extent of the interrelationships among the component parts of an organization.

These interrelationships are often just as vital as the specifications which an organization chart endeavors to indicate. Yet, if an organization chart were to be drawn with all the wide variety of criss-crossing communication and cooperation networks existent within a typical organization, the chart would probably be much more confusing than informative. It is also obvious that no organization chart as such can prove or disprove that the organizational structure it represents is effective in realizing the objectives of the organization. At best, an organization chart can only illustrate some of the various factors to be taken into consideration in understanding, devising, or altering organizational arrangements.

9. According to the above passage, an organization chart can be expected to portray the 9.____
   A. structure of the organization along somewhat ideal lines
   B. relative size of the organizational units quite accurately
   C. channels of information distribution within the organization graphically
   D. extent of the obligation of each unit to meet the organizational objectives

10. According to the above passage, those aspects of internal functioning which are NOT shown on an organization chart 10.____
   A. can be considered to have little practical application in the operations of the organization
   B. might well be considered to be as important as the structural relationships which a chart does present
   C. could be the cause of considerable confusion in the operations of an organization which is quite large
   D. would be most likely to provide the information needed to determine the overall effectiveness of an organization

11. In the above passage, the one of the following conditions which is NOT implied as being a defect of an organization chart is that an organization chart may 11.____
   A. present a picture of the organizational structure which is different from the structure that actually exists
   B. fail to indicate the comparative size of various organizational units
   C. be limited in its ability to convey some of the meaningful aspects of organizational relationships
   D. become less useful over a period of time during which the organizational facts which it illustrated have changed

12. The one of the following which is the MOST suitable title for the above passage is 12.____
   A. The Design and Construction of an Organization Chart
   B. The Informal Aspects of an Organization Chart
   C. The Inherent Deficiencies of an Organization Chart
   D. The Utilization of a Typical Organization Chart

13. It can be inferred from the above passage that the function of an organization chart is to 13.____
   A. contribute to the comprehension of the organization form and arrangements
   B. establish the capabilities of the organization to operate effectively
   C. provide a balanced picture of the operations of the organization
   D. eliminate the need for complexity in the organization's structure

Questions 14-16.

DIRECTIONS: Questions 14 through 16 are to be answered SOLELY on the basis of the following passage.

In dealing with visitors to the school office, the school secretary must use initiative, tact, and good judgment. All visitors should be greeted promptly and courteously. The nature of their business should be determined quickly and handled expeditiously. Frequently, the secretary should be able to handle requests, deliveries, or passes herself. Her judgment should determine when a visitor should see members of the staff or the principal. Serious problems or doubtful cases should be referred to a supervisor.

14. In general, visitors should be handled by the 14.____
   A. school secretary
   B. principal
   C. appropriate supervisor
   D. person who is free

15. It is wise to obtain the following information from visitors: 15.____
   A. Name
   B. Nature of business
   C. Address
   D. Problems they have

16. All visitors who wish to see members of the staff should 16.____
   A. be permitted to do so
   B. produce identification
   C. do so for valid reasons only
   D. be processed by a supervisor

Questions 17-19.

DIRECTIONS: Questions 17 through 19 are to be answered SOLELY on the basis of the following passage.

Information regarding payroll status, salary differentials, promotional salary increments, deductions, and pension payments should be given to all members of the staff who have questions regarding these items. On occasion, if the secretary is uncertain regarding the information, the staff member should be referred to the principal or the appropriate agency. No question by a staff member regarding payroll status should be brushed aside as immaterial or irrelevant. The school secretary must always try to handle the question or pass it on to the person who can handle it.

17. If a teacher is dissatisfied with information regarding her salary status, as given by the school secretary, the matter should be 17.____
   A. dropped
   B. passed on to the principal
   C. passed on by the secretary to proper agency or the principal
   D. made a basis for grievance procedures

18. The following is an adequate summary of the above passage: 18.____
   A. The secretary must handle all payroll matters
   B. The secretary must handle all payroll matter or know who can handle them
   C. The secretary or the principal must handle all payroll matters
   D. Payroll matter too difficult to handle must be followed up until they are solved

19. The above passage implies that 19.____
    A. many teachers ask immaterial questions regarding payroll status
    B. few teachers ask irrelevant pension questions
    C. no teachers ask immaterial salary questions
    D. no question regarding salary should be considered irrelevant

Questions 20-22.

DIRECTIONS: Questions 20 through 22 are to be answered SOLELY on the basis of the following passage.

The necessity for good speech on the part of the school secretary cannot be overstated. The school secretary must deal with the general public, the pupils, the members of the staff, and the school supervisors. In every situation which involves the general public, the secretary serves as a representative of the school. In dealing with pupils, the secretary's speech must serve as a model from which students may guide themselves. Slang, colloquialisms, malapropisms, and local dialects must be avoided.

20. The above passage implies that the speech pattern of the secretary must be 20.____
    A. perfect
    B. very good
    C. average
    D. on a level with that of the pupils

21. The last sentence indicates that slang 21.____
    A. is acceptable
    B. occurs in all speech
    C. might be used occasionally
    D. should be shunned

22. The above passage implies that the speech of pupils 22.____
    A. may be influenced
    B. does not change readily
    C. is generally good
    D. is generally poor

Questions 23-25.

DIRECTIONS: Questions 23 through 25 are to be answered SOLELY on the basis of the following passage.

The school secretary who is engaged in the task of filing records and correspondence should follow a general set of rules. Items which are filed should be available to other secretaries or to supervisors quickly and easily by means of the application of a modicum of common sense and good judgment. Items which, by their nature, may be difficult to find should be cross-indexed. Folders and drawers should be neatly and accurately labeled. There should never be a large accumulation of papers which have not been filed.

23. A good general rule to follow in filing is that materials should be 23.____
    A. placed in folders quickly
    B. neatly stored
    C. readily available
    D. cross-indexed

24. Items that are filed should be available to 24.____
    A. the secretary charged with the task of filing
    B. secretaries and supervisors
    C. school personnel
    D. the principal

25. A modicum of common sense means _____ common sense. 25.____
    A. an average amount of
    B. a great deal of
    C. a little
    D. no

KEY (CORRECT ANSWERS)

1.	B	11.	D
2.	A	12.	C
3.	C	13.	A
4.	C	14.	A
5.	D	15.	B
6.	B	16.	C
7.	B	17.	C
8.	C	18.	B
9.	A	19.	D
10.	B	20.	B

21. D
22. A
23. C
24. B
25. C

TEST 3

DIRECTIONS: Each question or incomplete statement is followed by several suggested answers or completions. Select the one that BEST answers the question or completes the statement. *PRINT THE LETTER OF THE CORRECT ANSWER IN THE SPACE AT THE RIGHT.*

Questions 1-4.

DIRECTIONS: Questions 1 through 4 are to be answered SOLELY on the basis of the following passage.

The proposition that administrative activity is essentially the same in all organizations appears to underlie some of the practices in the administration of private higher education. Although the practice is unusual in public education, there are numerous instances of industrial, governmental, or military administrators being assigned to private institutions of higher education and, to a lesser extent, of college and university presidents assuming administrative positions in other types of organizations. To test this theory that administrators are interchangeable, there is a need for systematic observation and classification. The myth that an educational administrator must first have experience in the teaching profession is firmly rooted in a long tradition that has historical prestige. The myth is bound up in the expectations of the public and personnel surrounding the administrator. Since administrative success depends significantly on how well an administrator meets the expectations others have of him, the myth may be more powerful than the special experience in helping the administrator attain organizational and educational objectives. Educational administrators who have risen through the teaching profession have often expressed nostalgia for the life of a teacher or scholar, but there is no evidence that this nostalgia contributes to administrative success.

1. Which of the following statements as completed is MOST consistent with the above passage? 1.____
   The greatest number of administrators has moved from
   A. industry and the military to government and universities
   B. government and universities to industry and the military
   C. government, the armed forces, and industry to colleges and universities
   D. colleges and universities to government, the armed forces, and industry

2. Of the following, the MOST reasonable inference from the above passage is that a specific area requiring further research is the 2.____
   A. place of myth in the tradition and history of the educational profession
   B. relative effectiveness of educational administrators from inside and outside the teaching profession
   C. performance of administrators in the administration of public colleges
   D. degree of reality behind the nostalgia for scholarly pursuits often expressed by educational administrators

3. According to the above passage, the value to an educational administrator of experience in the teaching profession 3.____
   A. lies in the first-hand knowledge he has acquired of immediate educational problems
   B. may lie in the belief of his colleagues, subordinates, and the public that such experience is necessary
   C. has been supported by evidence that the experience contributes to administrative success in educational fields
   D. would be greater if the administrator were able to free himself from nostalgia for his former duties

4. Of the following, the MOST suitable title for the above passage is 4.____
   A. Educational Administration, Its Problems
   B. The Experience Needed For Educational Administration
   C. Administration in Higher Education
   D. Evaluating Administrative Experience

Questions 5-6.

DIRECTIONS: Questions 5 and 6 are to be answered SOLELY on the basis of the following passage.

Management by objectives (MBO) may be defined as the process by which the superior and the subordinate managers of an organization jointly define its common goals, define each individual's major areas of responsibility in terms of the results expected of him and use these measure as guides for operating the unit and assessing the contribution of each of its members.

The MBO approach requires that after organizational goals are established and communicated, targets must be set for each individual position which are congruent with organizational goals. Periodic performance reviews and a final review using the objectives set as criteria are also basic to this approach.

Recent studies have shown that MBO programs are influenced by attitudes and perceptions of the boss, the company, the reward-punishment system, and the program itself. In addition, the manner in which the MBO program is carried out can influence the success of the program. A study done in the late sixties indicates that the best results are obtained when the manager sets goals which deal with significant problem areas in the organizational unit, or with the subordinate's personal deficiencies. These goals must be clear with regard to what is expected of the subordinate. The frequency of feedback is also important in the success of a management-by-objectives program. Generally, the greater the amount of feedback, the more successful the MBO program.

5. According to the above passage, the expected output for individual employees should be determined 5.____
   A. after a number of reviews of work performance
   B. after common organizational goals are defined
   C. before common organizational goals are defined
   D. on the basis of an employee's personal qualities

6. According to the above passage, the management-by-objectives approach requires 6.____
   A. less feedback than other types of management programs
   B. little review of on-the-job performance after the initial setting of goals
   C. general conformance between individual goals and organizational goals
   D. the setting of goals which deal with minor problem areas in the organization

Questions 7-10.

DIRECTIONS: Questions 7 through 10 are to be answered SOLELY on the basis of the following passage.

Management, which is the function of executive leadership, has as its principal phases the planning, organizing, and controlling of the activities of subordinate groups in the accomplishment of organizational objectives. Planning specifies the kind and extent of the factors, forces, and effects, and the relationships among them, that will be required for satisfactory accomplishment. The nature of the objectives and their requirements must be known before determinations can be made as to what must be done, how it must be done and why, where actions should take place, who should be responsible, and similar programs pertaining to the formulation of a plan. Organizing, which creates the conditions that must be present before the execution of the plan can be undertaken successfully, cannot be done intelligently without knowledge of the organizational objectives. Control, which has to do with the constraint and regulation of activities entering into the execution of the plan, must be exercised in accordance with the characteristics and requirements of the activities demanded by the plan.

7. The one of the following which is the MOST suitable title for the above passage is 7.____
   A. The Nature of Successful Organization
   B. The Planning of Management Functions
   C. The Importance of Organizational Functions
   D. The Principle Aspects of Management

8. It can be inferred from the above passage that the one of the following functions whose existence is essential to the existence of the other three is the 8.____
   A. regulation of the work needed to carry out a plan
   B. understanding of what the organization intends to accomplish
   C. securing of information of the factors necessary for accomplishment of objectives
   D. establishment of the conditions required for successful action

9. The one of the following which would NOT be included within any of the principal phases of the function of executive leadership as defined in the above passage is 9.____
   A. determination of manpower requirements
   B. procurement of required material
   C. establishment of organizational objectives
   D. scheduling of production

10. The conclusion which can MOST reasonably be drawn from the above passage is that the control phase of managing is most directly concerned with the 10.____
    A. influencing of policy determinations
    B. administering of suggestion systems
    C. acquisition of staff for the organization
    D. implementation of performance standards

Questions 11-12.

DIRECTIONS: Questions 11 and 12 are to be answered SOLELY on the basis of the following passage.

Under an open-and-above-board policy, it is to be expected that some supervisors will gloss over known shortcomings of subordinates rather than face the task of discussing team face-to-face. It is also to be expected that at least some employees whose job performance is below par will reject the supervisor's appraisal as biased and unfair. Be that as it may, these are inescapable aspects of any performance appraisal system in which human beings are involved. The supervisor who shies away from calling a spade a spade, as well as the employee with a chip on his shoulder, will each in his own way eventually be revealed in his true light—to the benefit of the organization as a whole.

11. The BEST of the following interpretations of the above passage is that 11.____
    A. the method of rating employee performance requires immediate revision to improve employee acceptance
    B. substandard performance ratings should be discussed with employees even if satisfactory ratings are not
    C. supervisors run the risk of being called unfair by the subordinates even though their appraisals are accurate
    D. any system of employee performance rating is satisfactory if used properly

12. The BEST of the following interpretations of the above passage is that 12.____
    A. supervisors generally are not open-and-above-board with their subordinates
    B. it is necessary for supervisors to tell employees objectively how they are performing
    C. employees complain when their supervisor does not keep them informed
    D. supervisors are afraid to tell subordinates their weaknesses

Questions 13-15.

DIRECTIONS: Questions 13 through 15 are to be answered SOLELY on the basis of the following passage.

During the last decade, a great deal of interest has been generated around the phenomenon of *organizational development,* or the process of developing human resources through conscious organization effort. Organizational development (OD) stresses improving interpersonal relationships and organizational skills, such as communication, to a much greater degree than individual training ever did. The kind of training that an organization should emphasize depends upon the present and future structure of the organization. If future organizations are to be unstable, shifting coalitions, then individual skills and abilities, particularly those emphasizing innovativeness, creativity, flexibility, and the latest technological knowledge, are crucial and individual training is most appropriate.

But if there is to be little change in organizational structure, then the main thrust of training should be group-oriented or organizational development. This approach seems better designed for overcoming hierarchical barriers, for developing a degree of interpersonal relationships which make communication along the chain of command possible, and for retaining a modicum of innovation and/or flexibility.

13. According to the above passage, group-oriented training is MOST useful in in 13.____
    A. developing a communications system that will facilitate understanding through the chain of command
    B. highly flexible and mobile organizations
    C. preventing the crossing of hierarchical barriers within an organization
    D. saving energy otherwise wasted on developing methods of dealing with rigid hierarchies

14. The one of the following conclusions which can be drawn MOST appropriately from the above passage is that 14.____
    A. behavioral research supports the use of organizational development training methods rather than individualized training
    B. it is easier to provide individualized training in specific skills than to set up sensitivity training programs
    C. organizational development eliminates innovative or flexible activity
    D. the nature of an organization greatly influences which training methods will be most effective

15. According to the above passage, the one of the following which is LEAST important for large-scale organizations geared to rapid and abrupt change is 15.____
    A. current technological information
    B. development of a high degree of interpersonal relationships
    C. development of individual skills and abilities
    D. emphasis on creativity

Questions 16-18.

DIRECTIONS: Questions 16 through 18 are to be answered SOLELY on the basis of the following passage.

The increase in the extent to which each individual is personally responsible to others is most noticeable in a large bureaucracy. No one person *decides* anything; each decision of any importance, is the product of an intricate process of brokerage involving individuals inside and outside the organization who feel some reason to be affected by the decision, or two have special knowledge to contribute to it. The more varied the organization's constituency, the more inside *veto-groups* will need to be taken into account. But even if no outside consultations were involved, sheer size would produce a complex process of decision. For a large organization is a deliberately created system of tensions into which each individual is expected to bring work-ways, viewpoints, and outside relationships markedly different from those of his colleagues. It is the administrator's task to draw from these disparate forces the elements of wise action from day to day, consistent with the purposes of the organization as a whole.

16. The above passage is essentially a description of decision-making as 16.____
    A. an organization process
    B. the key responsibility of the administrator
    C. the one best position among many
    D. a complex of individual decisions

17. Which one of the following statements BEST describes the responsibilities of an administrator? 17.____
    A. He modifies decisions and goals in accordance with pressures from within and outside the organization.
    B. He creates problem-solving mechanisms that rely on the varied interests of his staff and *veto-groups*.
    C. He makes determinations that will lead to attainment of his agency's objectives.
    D. He obtains agreement among varying viewpoints and interests

18. In the context of the operations of a central public personnel agency, a *veto-group* would LEAST likely consist of 18.____
    A. employee organizations
    B. professional personnel societies
    C. using agencies
    D. civil service newspapers

Questions 19-25.

DIRECTIONS: Questions 19 through 25 are to be answered SOLELY on the basis of the following passage, which is an extract from a report prepared for Department X, which outlines the procedure to be followed in the case of transfers of employees.

Every transfer, regardless of the reason therefore, requires completion of the record of transfer, Form DT411. To denote consent to the transfer, DT411 should contain the signatures of the transferee and the personnel officer(s) concerned, except that, in the case of an involuntary transfer, the signatures of the transferee's present and prospective supervisors shall be entered in Boxes 8A and 8B, respectively, since the transferee does not consent. Only a permanent employee may request a transfer; in such cases, the employee's attendance record shall be duly considered with regard to absences, latenesses, and accrued overtime balances. In the case of an inter-district transfer, the employee's attendance record must be included in Section 8A of the transfer request, Form DT410, by the personnel officer of the district from which the transfer is requested. The personnel officer of the district to which the employee requested transfer may refuse to accept accrued overtime balances in excess of ten days.

An employee on probation shall be eligible for transfer. If such employee is involuntarily transferred, he shall be credited for the period of time already served on probation. However, if such transfer is voluntary, the employee shall be required to serve the entire period of his probation in the new position. An employee who has occurred a disability which prevents him from performing his normal duties may be transferred during the period of such disability to other appropriate duties. A disability transfer requires the completion of either DT414 if the disability is job-connected, or Form DT415 if it is not a job-connected disability. In either case, the personnel officer of the district from which the transfer is made signs in Box 6A of the first two copies and the personnel officer of the district to which the transfer is made signs in Box 6B of the last two copies, or, in the case of an intra-district disability transfer, the personnel officer must sign in Box 6A of the first two copies and Box 6B of the last two copies.

19. When a personnel officer consents to an employee's request for transfer from his district, this procedure requires that the personnel officer sign Forms 19.____
    A. DT411
    B. DT410 and DT411
    C. DT411 and either Form DT414 or DT415
    D. DT410 and DT411, and either Form DT414 or DT415

20. With respect to the time record of an employee transferred against his wishes during his probationary period, this procedure requires that 20.____
    A. he serve the entire period of his probation in his present office
    B. he lose his accrued overtime balance
    C. his attendance record be considered with regard to absences and latenesses
    D. he be given credit for the period of time he has already served on probation

21. Assume you are a supervisor and an employee must be transferred into your office against his wishes. 21.____
    According to this procedure, the box you must sign on the record of transfer is
    A. 6A   B. 8A   C. 6B   D. 8B

22. Under this procedure, in the case of a disability transfer, when must Box 6A on Forms DT414 and DT415 be signed by the personnel officer of the district to which the transfer is being made? 22.____
    A. In all cases when either Form DT414 or Form DT415 is used
    B. In all cases when Form DT414 is used and only under certain circumstances when Form DT415 is used
    C. In all cases when Form DT415 is used and only under certain circumstances when Form DT414 is used
    D. Only under certain circumstances when either Form DT414 or Form DT415 is used

23. From the above passage, it may be inferred MOST correctly that the number of copies of Form DT414 is 23.____
    A. no more than 2
    B. at least 3
    C. at least 5
    D. more than the number of copies of Form DT415

24. A change in punctuation and capitalization only which would change one sentence into two and possibly contribute to somewhat greater ease of reading this report extract would be MOST appropriate in the 24.____
    A. 2nd sentence, 1st paragraph
    B. 3rd sentence, 1st paragraph
    C. next to the last sentence, 2nd paragraph
    D. 2nd sentence, 2nd paragraph

25. In the second paragraph, a word that is INCORRECTLY used is 25.____
    A. *shall* in the 1st sentence
    B. *voluntary* in the 3rd sentence
    C. *occurred* in the 4th sentence
    D. *intra-district* in the last sentence

KEY (CORRECT ANSWERS)

1.	C	11.	C
2.	B	12.	B
3.	B	13.	A
4.	B	14.	D
5.	B	15.	B
6.	C	16.	A
7.	D	17.	C
8.	B	18.	B
9.	C	19.	A
10.	D	20.	D

21.	D
22.	D
23.	B
24.	B
25.	C

COMMUNICATION

EXAMINATION SECTION
TEST 1

DIRECTIONS: Each question or incomplete statement is followed by several suggested answers or completions. Select the one that BEST answers the question or completes the statement. *PRINT THE LETTER OF THE CORRECT ANSWER IN THE SPACE AT THE RIGHT.*

1. In some agencies the counsel to the agency head is given the right to bypass the chain of command and issue orders directly to the staff concerning matters that involve certain specific processes and practices. 1.____
This situation MOST nearly illustrates the principle of _____ authority.
   A. the acceptance theory of
   B. multiple-linear
   C. splintered
   D. functional

2. It is commonly understood that communication is an important part of the administrative process. 2.____
Which of the following is NOT a valid principle of the communication process in administration?
   A. The channels of communication should be spontaneous.
   B. The lines of communication should be as direct and as short as possible.
   C. Communications should be authenticated.
   D. The persons serving in communications centers should be competent.

3. Of the following, the one factor which is generally considered LEAST essential to successful committee operations is 3.____
   A. stating a clear definition of the authority and scope of the committee
   B. selecting the committee chairman carefully
   C. limiting the size of the committee to four persons
   D. limiting the subject matter to that which can be handled in group discussion

4. Of the following, the failure by line managers to accept and appreciate the benefits and limitations of a new program or system VERY FREQUENTLY can be traced to the 4.____
   A. budgetary problems involved
   B. resultant need to reduce staff
   C. lack of controls it engenders
   D. failure of top management to support its implementation

5. If a manager were thinking about using a committee of subordinates to solve an operating problem, which of the following would generally NOT be an advantage of such use of the committee approach? 5.____
   A. Improved coordination
   B. Low cost
   C. Increased motivation
   D. Integrated judgment

6. Every supervisor has many occasions to lead a conference or participate in a conference of some sort. 6.____
Of the following statements that pertain to conferences and conference leadership, which is generally considered to be MOST valid?
   A. Since World War II, the trend has been toward fewer shared decisions and more conferences.
   B. The most important part of a conference leader's job is to direct discussion.
   C. In providing opportunities for group interaction, management should avoid consideration of its past management philosophy.
   D. A good administrator cannot lead a good conference if he is a poor public speaker.

7. Of the following, it is usually LEAST desirable for a conference leader to 7.____
   A. call the name of a person after asking a question
   B. summarize proceedings periodically
   C. make a practice of repeating questions
   D. ask a question without indicating who is to reply

8. Assume that, in a certain organization, a situation has developed in which there is little difference in status or authority between individuals. 8.____
Which of the following would be the MOST likely result with regard to communication in this organization?
   A. Both the accuracy and flow of communication will be improved.
   B. Both the accuracy and flow of communication will substantially decrease.
   C. Employees will seek more formal lines of communication.
   D. Neither the flow nor the accuracy of communication will be improved over the former hierarchical structure.

9. The main function of many agency administrative officers is "information management." Information that is received by an administrative officer may be classified as active or passive, depending upon whether or not it requires the recipient to take some action. 9.____
Of the following, the item received which is clearly the MOST active information is
   A. an appointment of a new staff member
   B. a payment voucher for a new desk
   C. a press release concerning a past event
   D. the minutes of a staff meeting

10. Of the following, the one LEAST considered to be a communication barrier is 10.____
   A. group feedback
   B. charged words
   C. selective perception
   D. symbolic meanings

11. Management studies support the hypothesis that, in spite of the tendency of employees to censor the information communicated to their supervisor, subordinates are more likely to communicate problem-oriented information UPWARD when they have a 11.____
   A. long period of service in the organization
   B. high degree of trust in the supervisor
   C. high educational level
   D. low status on the organizational ladder

12. Electronic data processing equipment can produce more information faster than can be generated by any other means. 12.____
In view of this, the MOST important problem faced by management at present is to
   A. keep computers fully occupied
   B. find enough computer personnel
   C. assimilate and properly evaluate the information
   D. obtain funds to establish appropriate information systems

13. A well-designed management information system essentially provides each executive and manager the information he needs for 13.____
   A. determining computer time requirements
   B. planning and measuring results
   C. drawing a new organization chart
   D. developing a new office layout

14. It is generally agreed that management policies should be periodically reappraised and restated in accordance with current conditions. 14.____
Of the following, the approach which would be MOST effective in determining whether a policy should be revised is to
   A. conduct interviews with staff members at all levels in order to ascertain the relationship between the policy and actual practice
   B. make proposed revisions in the policy and apply it to current problems
   C. make up hypothetical situations using both the old policy and a revised version in order to make comparisons
   D. call a meeting of top level staff in order to discuss ways of revising the policy

15. Your superior has asked you to notify division employees of an important change in one of the operating procedures described in the division manual. Every employee presently has a copy of this manual. 15.____
Which of the following is normally the MOST practical way to get the employees to understand such a change?
   A. Notify each employee individually of the change and answer any questions he might have
   B. Send a written notice to key personnel, directing them to inform the people under them

C. Call a general meeting, distribute a corrected page for the manual, and discuss the change
D. Send a memo to employees describing the change in general terms and asking them to make the necessary corrections in their copies of the manual

16. Assume that the work in your department involves the use of any technical terms. 16.____
In such a situation, when you are answering inquiries from the general public, it would usually be BEST to
A. use simple language and avoid the technical terms
B. employ the technical terms whenever possible
C. bandy technical terms freely, but explain each term in parentheses
D. apologize if you are forced to use a technical term

17. Suppose that you receive a telephone call from someone identifying himself as an employee in another city department who asks to be given information which your own department regards as confidential. 17.____
Which of the following is the BEST way of handling such a request?
A. Give the information requested, since your caller as official standing
B. Grant the request, provided the caller gives you a signed receipt
C. Refuse the request, because you have no way of knowing whether the caller is really who he claims to be
D. Explain that the information is confidential and inform the caller of the channels he must go through to have the information released to him

18. Studies show that office employees place high importance on the social and human aspects of the organization. What office employees like best about their jobs is the kind of people with whom they work. So strive hard to group people who are most likely to get along well together. 18.____
Based on this information, it is MOST reasonable to assume that office workers are most pleased to work in a group which
A. is congenial
B. has high productivity
C. allows individual creativity
D. is unlike other groups

19. A certain supervisor does not compliment members of his staff when they come up with good ideas. He feels that coming up with good ideas is part of the job and does not merit special attention. 19.____
This supervisor's practice is
A. *poor*, because recognition for good ideas is a good motivator
B. *poor*, because the staff will suspect that the supervisor has no good ideas of his own
C. *good*, because it is reasonable to assume that employees will tell their supervisor of ways to improve office practice
D. *good*, because the other members of the staff are not made to seem inferior by comparison

20. Some employees of a department have sent an anonymous letter containing many complaints to the department head. 20.____
Of the following, what is this MOST likely to show about the department?
    A. It is probably a good place to work.
    B. Communications are probably poor.
    C. The complaints are probably unjustified.
    D. These employees are probably untrustworthy.

21. Which of the following actions would usually be MOST appropriate for a supervisor to take after receiving an instruction sheet from his superior explaining a new procedure which is to be followed? 21.____
    A. Put the instruction sheet aside temporarily until he determines what is wrong with the old procedure.
    B. Call his superior and ask whether the procedure is one he must implement immediately.
    C. Write a memorandum to the superior asking for more details.
    D. Try the new procedure and advise the superior of any problems or possible improvements.

22. Of the following, which one is considered the PRIMARY advantage of using a committee to resolved a problem in an organization? 22.____
    A. No one person will be held accountable for the decision since a group of people was involved.
    B. People with different backgrounds give attention to the problem.
    C. The decision will take considerable time so there is unlikely to be a decision that will later be regretted.
    D. One person cannot dominate the decision-making process.

23. Employees in a certain office come to their supervisor with all their complaints about the office and the work. Almost every employee has had at least one minor complaint at some time. 23.____
The situation with respect to complaints in this office may BEST be described as probably
    A. *good*; employees who complain care about their jobs and work hard
    B. *good*; grievances brought out into the open can be corrected
    C. *bad*; only serious complaints should be discussed
    D. *bad*; it indicates the staff does not have confidence in the administration

24. The administrator who allows his staff to suggest ways to do their work will usually find that 24.____
    A. this practice contributes to high productivity
    B. the administrator's ideas produce greater output
    C. clerical employees suggest inefficient work methods
    D. subordinate employees resent performing a management function

25. The MAIN purpose for a supervisor's questioning the employees at a conference he is holding is to 25.____
    A. stress those areas of information covered but not understood by the participants
    B. encourage participants to think through the problem under discussion
    C. catch those subordinates who are not paying attention
    D. permit the more knowledgeable participants to display their grasp of the problems being discussed

---

KEY (CORRECT ANSWERS)

1. D
2. A
3. C
4. D
5. B

6. B
7. C
8. D
9. A
10. A

11. B
12. C
13. B
14. A
15. C

16. A
17. D
18. A
19. A
20. B

21. D
22. B
23. B
24. A
25. B

TEST 2

DIRECTIONS: Each question or incomplete statement is followed by several suggested answers or completions. Select the one that BEST answers the question or completes the statement. *PRINT THE LETTER OF THE CORRECT ANSWER IN THE SPACE AT THE RIGHT.*

1. For a superior to use *consultative supervision* with his subordinates effectively, it is ESSENTIAL that he 1.____
   A. accept the fact that his formal authority will be weakened by the procedure
   B. admit that he does not know more than all his men together and that his ideas are not always best
   C. utilize a committee system so that the procedure is orderly
   D. make sure that all subordinates are consulted so that no one feels left out

2. The *grapevine* is an informal means of communication in an organization. 2.____
   The attitude of a supervisor with respect to the grapevine should be to
   A. ignore it since it deals mainly with rumors and sensational information
   B. regard it as a serious danger which should be eliminated
   C. accept it as a real line of communication which should be listened to
   D. utilize it for most purposes instead of the official line of communication

3. The supervisor of an office that must deal with the public should realize that planning in this type of work situation 3.____
   A. is useless because he does not know how many people will request service or what service they will request
   B. must be done at a higher level but that he should be ready to implement the results of such planning
   C. is useful primarily for those activities that are not concerned with public contact
   D. is useful for all the activities of the office, including those that relate to public contact

4. Assume that it is your job to receive incoming telephone calls. Those calls which you cannot handle yourself have to be transferred to the appropriate office. 4.____
   If you receive an outside call for an extension line which is busy, the one of the following which you should do FIRST is to
   A. interrupt the person speaking on the extension and tell him a call is waiting
   B. tell the caller the line is busy and let him know every thirty seconds whether or not it is free
   C. leave the caller on "hold" until the extension is free
   D. tell the caller the line is busy and ask him if he wishes to wait

5. Your superior has subscribed to several publications directly related to your division's work, and he has asked you to see to it that the publications are circulated among the supervisory personnel in the division. There are eight supervisors involved. 5.____
The BEST method of insuring that all eight see these publications is to
   A. place the publication in the division's general reference library as soon as it arrives
   B. inform each supervisor whenever a publication arrives and remind all of them that they are responsible for reading it
   C. prepare a standard slip that can be stapled to each publication, listing the eight supervisors and saying, "Please read, initial your name, and pass along"
   D. send a memo to the eight supervisors saying that they may wish to purchase individual subscriptions in their own names if they are interested in seeing each issue

6. Your superior has telephoned a number of key officials in your agency to ask whether they can meet at a certain time next month. He has found that they can all make it, and he has asked you to confirm the meeting. 6.____
Which of the following is the BEST way to confirm such a meeting?
   A. Note the meeting on your superior's calendar.
   B. Post a notice of the meeting on the agency bulletin board.
   C. Call the officials on the day of the meeting to remind them of the meeting.
   D. Write a memo to each official involved, repeating the time and place of the meeting.

7. Assume that a new city regulation requires that certain kinds of private organizations file information forms with your department. You have been asked to write the short explanatory message that will be printed on the front cover of the pamphlet containing the forms and instructions. 7.____
Which of the following would be the MOST appropriate way of beginning this message?
   A. Get the readers' attention by emphasizing immediately that there are legal penalties for organizations that fail to file before a certain date.
   B. Briefly state the nature of the enclosed forms and the types of organizations that must file.
   C. Say that your department is very sorry to have to put organizations to such an inconvenience.
   D. Quote the entire regulation adopted by the city, even if it is quite long and is expressed din complicated legal language.

8. Suppose that you have been told to make up the vacation schedule for the 18 employees in a particular unit. In order for the unit to operate effectively, only a few employees can be on vacation at the same time. 8.____
Which of the following is the MOST advisable approach in making up the schedule?
   A. Draw up a schedule assigning vacations in alphabetical order
   B. Find out when the supervisors want to take their vacations, and randomly assign whatever periods are left to the non-supervisory personnel

C. Assign the most desirable times to employees of longest standing and the least desirable times to the newest employees
D. Have all employees state their own preference, and then work out any conflicts in consultation with the people involved

9. Assume that you have been asked to prepare job descriptions for various positions in your department. 9.____
Which of the following are the basic points that should be covered in a *job description*?
A. General duties and responsibilities of the position, with examples of day-to-day tasks
B. Comments on the performances of present employees
C. Estimates of the number of openings that may be available in each category during the coming year
D. Instructions for carrying out the specific tasks assigned to your department

10. Of the following, the biggest DISADVANTAGE in allowing a free flow of communications in an agency is that such a free flow 10.____
A. decreases creativity
B. increases the use of the *grapevine*
C. lengthens the chain of command
D. reduces the executive's power to direct the flow of information

11. A downward flow of authority in an organization is one example of _____ communication. 11.____
A. horizontal B. informal C. circular D. vertical

12. Of the following, the one that would MOST likely block effective communication is 12.____
A. concentration only on the issues at hand
B. lack of interest or commitment
C. use of written reports
D. use of charts and graphs

13. An ADVANTAGE of the *lecture* as a teaching tool is that it 13.____
A. enables a person to present his ideas to a large number of people
B. allows the audience to retain a maximum of the information given
C. holds the attention of the audience for the longest time
D. enables the audience member to easily recall the main points

14. An ADVANTAGE of the *small-group* discussion as a teaching tool is that 14.____
A. it always focuses attention on one person as the leader
B. it places collective responsibility on the group as a whole
C. its members gain experience by summarizing the ideas of others
D. each member of the group acts as a member of a team

15. The one of the following that is an ADVANTAGE of a *large-group* discussion, when compared to a small-group discussion, is that the large-group discussion 15.____
    A. moves along more quickly than a small-group discussion
    B. allows its participants to feel more at ease, and speak out more freely
    C. gives the whole group a chance to exchange ideas on a certain subject at the same occasion
    D. allows its members to feel a greater sense of personal responsibility

KEY (CORRECT ANSWERS)

1.	D	6.	D	11.	D
2.	C	7.	B	12.	B
3.	D	8.	D	13.	A
4.	D	9.	A	14.	D
5.	C	10.	D	15.	C

PREPARING WRITTEN MATERIAL

EXAMINATION SECTION

TEST 1

DIRECTIONS: Each short paragraph below is followed by four restatements or summaries of the information contained within it. Select the one that most completely and accurately restates the information given in the paragraph. *PRINT THE LETTER OF THE CORRECT ANSWER IN THE SPACE AT THE RIGHT.*

1. India's night jasmine, or hurshinghar, is different from most flowering plants, in that its flowers are closed during the day, and open after dark. The scientific reason for this is probably that the plant has avoided competing with other flowers for pollinating insects and birds, and relies instead on the service of nocturnal bats that are drawn to the flower's nectar. According to an old Indian legend, however, the flowers sprouted from the funeral ashes of a beautiful young girl who had fallen hopelessly in love with the sun. 1.____
   A. Despite the Indian legend that explains why the hurshinghar's flowers open at dusk, scientists believe it has to do with competition for available pollinators.
   B. The Indian hurshinghar's closure of its flowers during the day is due to a lack of available pollinators.
   C. The hurshinghar of India has evolved an unhealthy dependency on nocturnal bats.
   D. Like most myths, the Indian legend of the hurshinghar's night-flowering has been disproved by science.

2. Charles Lindbergh's trans-Atlantic flight from New York to Paris made him an international hero in 1927, but he lived nearly another fifty years, and by most accounts they weren't terribly happy ones. The two greatest tragedies of his life—the 1932 kidnapping and murder of his oldest son, and an unshakeable reputation as a Nazi sympathizer during World War II—he blamed squarely on the rabid media hounds who stalked his every move. 2.____
   A. Despite the fact that Charles Lindbergh had a hand in the two greatest tragedies of his life, he insisted on blaming the media for his problems.
   B. Charles Lindbergh lived a largely unhappy life after the glory of his 1927 trans-Atlantic flight, and he blamed his unhappiness on media attention
   C. Charles Lindbergh's later life was marked by despair and disillusionment.
   D. Because of the rabid media attention sparked by Charles Lindbergh's 1927 trans-Atlantic flight, he would later consider it the last happy event of his life

3. The United States, one of the world's youngest nations in the early twentieth century, had yet to spread its wings in terms of foreign affairs, preferring to remain isolated and opposed to meddling in the affairs of others. But the fact remained that as a young nation situated on the opposite side of the globe from Europe, Africa, and Asia, the United States had much work to do in 3.____

establishing relations with the rest of the world. So, too, as the European colonial powers continued to battle for influence in North and South America, did the United States come to believe that it was proper for them to keep these nations from encroaching into their sphere of influence.

A. The roots of the Monroe Doctrine can be traced to the foreign policy shift of the United States during the early nineteenth century.
B. In the early nineteenth century, the United States shifted its foreign policy to reflect a growing desire to actively protect its interests in the Western Hemisphere.
C. In the early nineteenth century, the United States was too young and undeveloped to have devised much in the way of foreign policy.
D. The United States adopted a more aggressive foreign policy in the early nineteenth century in order to become a diplomatic player on the world stage.

4. Hertha Ayrton, a nineteenth-century Englishwoman, pursued a career in science during a time when most women were not given the opportunity to go to college. Her series of successes led to her induction into the Institution of Electrical Engineers in 1899, when she was the first woman to receive this professional honor. Her most noted accomplishment was the research and invention of an anti-gas fan that the British War Office used in the trench warfare of World War I. 4.____

A. The British Army's success in World War I can be partly attributed to Hertha Ayrton, a groundbreaking British scientist.
B. Hertha Ayrton was the first woman to be inducted into the Institution of Electrical Engineers.
C. The injustices of nineteenth-century England were no match for the brilliant mind of Hertha Ayrton.
D. Hertha Ayrton defied the restrictions of her society by building a successful scientific career.

5. Scientists studying hyenas in Tanzania's Ngorongoro Crater have observed that hyena clans have evolved a system of territoriality that allows each clan a certain space to hunt within the 100-square-mile area. These territories are not marked by natural boundaries, but by droppings and excretions from the hyenas' scent glands. Usually, the hyenas take these boundary lines very seriously; some hyena clans have been observed abandoning their pursuit of certain prey after the prey has crossed into another territory, even though no members of the neighboring clan are anywhere in sight. 5.____

A. The hyenas of Ngorongoro Crater illustrate that the best way to peacefully co-exist within a limited territory is to strictly delineate and defend territorial borders.
B. While most territorial boundaries are marked using geographical features, the hyenas of Ngorongoro Crater have devised another method.
C. The hyena clans of Ngorongoro Crater, in order to co-exist within a limited hunting territory, have developed a method of marking strict territorial boundaries.
D. As with most species, the hyenas of Ngorongoro Crater have proven the age-old motto: "To the victor go the spoils."

6. The flood control policy of the U.S. Army Corps of Engineers has long been an obvious feature of the American landscape—the Corps seeks to contain the nation's rivers with an enormous network of dams and levees, "channelizing" rivers into small, confined routes that will stay clear of settled flood—plains when rivers rise. As a command of the U.S. Army, the Corps seems to have long seen the nation's rivers as an enemy to be fought; one of the agency's early training films speaks of the Corps' "battle" with its adversary, Mother Nature. 6.____
   A. The dams and levees built by the U.S. Army Corps of Engineers have at least defeated their adversary, Mother Nature.
   B. The flood control policy of the U.S. Army Corps of Engineers has often reflected a military point of view, making the nation's rivers into enemies that must be defeated.
   C. When one realizes that the flood policy of the U.S. Army Corps of Engineers has always relied on a kind of military strategy, it is only possible to view the Corps' efforts as a failure.
   D. By damming and channelizing the nation's rivers, the U.S. Army Corps of Engineers have made America's flood plains safe for farming and development.

7. Frogs with extra legs or missing legs have been showing up with greater frequency over the past decade, and scientists have been baffled by the cause. Some researchers have concluded that pesticide runoff from farms is to blame; others say a common parasite, the trematode, is the culprit. Now, a new study suggests that both these factors in combination have disturbed normal development in many frogs, leading to the abnormalities. 7.____
   A. Despite several studies, scientists still have no idea what is causing the widespread incidence of deformities among aquatic frogs.
   B. In the debate over what is causing the increase in frog deformities, environmentalists tend to blame pesticide runoff, while others blame a common parasite, the trematode.
   C. A recent study suggests that both pesticide runoff and natural parasites have contributed to the increasing rate of deformities in frogs.
   D. Because of their aquatic habitat, frogs are among the most susceptible organisms to chemical ad environmental change, and this is illustrated by the increasing rate of physical deformities among frog populations.

8. The builders of the Egyptian pyramids, to insure that each massive structure was built on a completely flat surface, began by cutting a network of criss-crossing channels into the pyramid's mapped-out ground space and partly filling the channels with water. Because the channels were all interconnected, the water was distributed evenly throughout the channel system, and all the workers had to do to level their building surface was cut away any rock above the waterline. 8.____
   A. The modern carpenter's level uses a principle that was actually invented several centuries ago by the builders of the Egyptian pyramids.
   B. The discovery of the ancient Egyptians' sophisticated construction techniques is a quiet argument against the idea that they were built by slaves.

C. The use of water to insure that the pyramids were level mark the Egyptians as one of the most scientifically advanced of the ancient civilizations.
D. The builders of the Egyptian pyramids used a simple but ingenious method for ensuring a level building surface with interconnected channels of water

9. Thunderhead Mountain, a six-hundred-foot-high formation of granite in the Black Hills of South Dakota, is slowly undergoing a transformation that will not be finished for more than a century, when what remains of the mountain will have become the largest sculpture in the world. The statue, begun in 1947 by a Boston Sculptor named Henry Ziolkowski, is still being carved and blasted by his wife and children into the likeness of Crazy Horse, the legendary chief of the Sioux tribe of American natives. The enormity of the sculpture—the planned length of one of the figure's arms is 263 feet—is understandable, given the historical greatness of Crazy Horse. 9.____
A. Only a hero as great as Crazy Horse could warrant a sculpture so large that it will take morae than a century to complete.
B. In 1947, sculptor Henry Ziolkowski began work on what he imagined would be the largest sculpture in the world—even though he knew he would not live to see it completed.
C. The huge Black Hills sculpture of the great Sioux chief Crazy Horse, still being carried out by the family of Henry Ziolkowski, will some day be the largest sculpture in the world.
D. South Dakota's Thunderhead Mountain will soon be the site of the world's largest sculpture, a statue of the Sioux chief Crazy Horse.

10. Because they were some of the first explorers to venture into the western frontier of North America, the French were responsible for the naming of several native tribes. Some of these names were poorly conceived—the worst of which was perhaps Eskimo, the name for the natives of the far North, which translates roughly as "eaters of raw flesh." The name is incorrect; these people have always cooked their fish and game, and they now call themselves the Inuit, a native term that means "the people." 10.____
A. The first to explore much of North America's western frontier were the French, and they usually gave improper or poorly-informed names to the native tribes.
B. The Eskimos of North America have never eaten raw flesh, so it is curious that the French would give them a name that means "eaters of raw flesh."
C. The Inuit have fought for many years to overcome the impression that they eat raw flesh.
D. Like many native tribes, the Inuit were once incorrectly named by French explorers, but they have since corrected the mistake themselves.

11. Of the 30,000 species of spiders worldwide, only a handful are dangerous to human beings, but this doesn't prevent many people from having a powerful fear of all spiders, whether they are venomous or not. The leading scientific theory about arachnophobia, as this fear is known, is that far in our evolutionary past, some species of spider must have presented a serious enough threat to people that the sight of a star-shaped body or an eight-legged walk was coded into our genes as a danger signal. 11.____
    A. Scientists theorize that peoples' widespread fear of spiders can be traced to an ancient spider species that was dangerous enough to trigger this fearful reaction.
    B. The fear known as arachnophobia is triggered by the sight of a star-shaped body or an eight-legged walk.
    C. Because most spiders have a uniquely shaped body that triggers a human fear response, many humans are afflicted with the fear of spiders known as arachnophobia.
    D. Though only a few of the planet's 30,000 spider species are dangerous to people, many people have an unreasonable fear of them.

12. From the 1970s to the 1990s, the percentage of Americans living in the suburbs climbed from 37% to 47%. In the latter part of the 1990s, a movement emerged that questioned the good of such a population shift—or at least, the good of the speed and manner in which this suburban land was being developed. Often, people began to argue, the planning of such growth was flawed, resulting in a phenomenon that has become known as suburban "sprawl," or the growth of suburban orbits around cities at rates faster than infrastructures could support, and in ways that are damaging to the environment 12.____
    A. The term "urban sprawl" was coined in the 1990s, when the movement against unchecked suburban development began to gather momentum.
    B. In the 1980s and 1990s, home builders benefited from a boom in their most favored demographic segment, suburban new home buyers.
    C. Suburban development tends to suffer from poor planning, which can lead to a lower quality of life for residents
    D. The surge in suburban residences in the late twentieth century was criticized by many as "sprawl" that could not be supported by existing resources

13. Medicare, a $200 billion-a-year program, processes 1 billion claims annually, and in the year 2000, the computer system that handles these claims came under criticism. The General Accounting Office branded Medicare's financial management system as outdated and inadequate—one in a series of studies and reports warning that the program is plagued with duplication, overcharges, double billings, and confusion among users. 13.____
    A. The General Accounting Office's 2000 report proves that Medicare is bloated bureaucracy in need of substantial reform.
    B. Medicare's confusing computer network is an example of how the federal government often neglects the programs that mean the most to average American citizens.

C. In the year 2000, the General Accounting Office criticized Medicare's financial accounting network as inefficient and outdated.
D. Because it has to handle so many claims each year, Medicare's financial accounting system often produces redundancies and errors.

14. The earliest known writing materials were thin clay tablets, used in Mesopotamia more than 5,000 years ago. Although the tablets were cheap and easy to produce, they had two major disadvantages: they were difficult to store, and once the clay had dried and hardened, a person could not write on them. The ancient Egyptians later discovered a better writing material—the thin bark of the papyrus reed, a plant that grew near the mouth of the Nile River, which could be peeled into long strips, woven into a mat-like layer, pounded flat with heavy mallets, and then dried in the sun. 14.____
A. The Egyptians, after centuries of frustration with clay writing tablets, were finally forced to invent a better writing surface.
B. With the bark of the papyrus reed, ancient Egyptians made a writing material that overcame the disadvantages of clay tablets.
C. The Egyptian invention of the papyrus scroll was necessitated in part by a relative lack of available clay.
D. The word "paper" can be traced to the innovations of the Egyptians, who made the first paper-like writing material from the bark of papyrus plant.

15. In 1850, the German pianomaker Heinrich Steinweg and his family stepped off an immigrant ship in New York City, threw themselves into competition with dozens of other established craftsmen, and defeated them all by reinventing the instrument. The company they created commanded the market for nearly the next century and a half, while their competitors—some of the most acclaimed pianomakers in the business—faded into obscurity. And all the while, Steinway & Sons, through their sponsorship and encouragement of the world's most distinguished pianists, helped define the cultural life of the young United States. 15.____
A. The Steinways capitalized on weak competition during the mid-nineteenth century to capture the American piano market.
B. Because of their technical and cultural innovations, the Steinways had an advantage over other American pianomakers.
C. Heinrich Steinweg founded the Steinway piano empire in 1850.
D. From humble immigrant origins, the Steinway family rose to dominate both the pianomaking industry and American musical culture.

16. Feng Shui, the ancient Chinese science of studying the natural environment's effect on a person's well-being, has gained new popularity in the design and decoration of buildings. Although a complex area of study, a basic premise of Feng Shui is that each building creates a unique field of energy which affects the inhabitants of that building or home. In recent years, decorators and realtors have begun to offer services which include a diagnosis of a building's Feng Shui, or energy. 16.____
A. Feng Shui, the Chinese science of balancing environmental energies, has been given more aesthetic quality by recent practitioners.

B. Generally, practitioners of Feng Shui work to create balance within a room, carefully arranging sharp and soft surfaces to create a positive environment that suits the room's primary purpose.
C. The idea behind the Chinese "science" of Feng Sui objects give off certain energies that affect a building's inhabitants has been a difficult one for most Westerners to accept, but it is gaining in popularity.
D. The ancient Chinese science of Feng Shui, which studies the balance of energies in a person's environment, has become popular among those who design and decorate buildings.

17. Because the harsh seasonal variations of the Kansas plains make survival difficult for most plant life, the area is dominated by tall, sturdy grasses. The only tree that has been able to survive and prosper throughout the wide expanse of prairie is the cottonwood, which can take root and grow in the most extreme climatic conditions. Sometimes a storm will shear off a living branch and carry it downstream, where it may snag along a sandbar and take root. 17.____
A. Among the plant life of the Kansas plains, the only tree is the cottonwood.
B. The only prosperous tree on the Kansas plains is the cottonwood, which can take root and grow in a wide range of conditions.
C. Only the cottonwood, whose branches can grow after being broken off and washed down a river, is capable of surviving the climatic extremes of the Kansas plains.
D. Because it is the most widespread and hardiest tree on the Kansas plains, the cottonwood had become a symbol of pioneer grit and fortitude.

18. In the twenty-first century, it's easy to see the automobile as the keystone of American popular culture. Subtract linen dusters, driving goggles, and women's *crepe de chine* veils from our history, and you've taken the Roaring out of the Twenties. Take away the ducktail haircuts, pegged pants, and upturned collars from the teen Car Cult of the Fifties, and the decade isn't nearly as Fabulous. Were the chromed and tailfinned muscle cars of the automobile' Golden Age modeled after us, or were we mimicking them? 18.____
A. Ever since its invention, the automobile has shaped American culture.
B. Many of the familiar names we give historical era, such as "Roaring Twenties" and "Fabulous Fifties," were given because of the predominance of the automobile.
C. Americans' tastes in clothing have been determined primarily by the cars they drive.
D. Teenagers have had a fascination for automobiles ever since the motorcar was first invented.

19. Since the 1960s, an important issue for Canada has been the status of minority French-speaking Canadians, especially in the province of Quebec, whose inhabitants make up 30% of the Canadian population and trace their ancestry back to a Canada that preceded British influence. In response to pressure from Quebec nationalists, the government in 1982 added a Charter of Rights to the constitution, restoring important rights that dated back to the time of aboriginal treaties. Separatism is still a prominent issue, though successive 19.____

referendums and constitutional inquiries have not resulted in any realistic progress toward Quebec's independence.

A. Despite the fact that Quebec's inhabitants have their roots in Canada's original settlers, they have been constantly oppressed by the descendants of those who came later, the British.
B. It seems unavoidable that Quebec's linguistic and cultural differences with the rest of Canada will some day lead to its secession.
C. French-speaking Quebec's activism over the last several decades has led to concessions by the Canadian government, but it seems that Quebec will remain a part of the country for some time.
D. The inhabitants of Quebec are an aboriginal culture that has been exploited by the Canadian government for years, but they are gradually winning back their rights.

20. For years, musicians and scientists have tried to discover what it is about an eighteenth-century Stradivarius violin—which may sell for more than $1 million on today's market—that gives it its unique sound. In 1977, American scientist Joseph Nagyvary discovered that the Stradivarius is made of a spruce wood that came from Venice, where timber was stored beneath the sea, and unlike the dry-seasoned wood from which other violins were made, this spruce contains microscopic holes which add resonance to the violin's sound. Nagyvary also found the varnish used on the Stradivarius to be equally unique, containing tiny mineral crystals that appear to have come from ground-up gemstones, which would filter out high-pitched tones and give the violin a smoother sound. 20.____

A. After carefully studying Stradivarius violins to discover the source of their unique sound, an American scientist discovered two qualities in the construction of them that set them apart from other instruments: the wood from which they were made, and the varnish used to coat the wood.
B. The two qualities that give the Stradivarius violin such a unique sound are the wood, which adds resonance, and the finish, which filters out high-pitched tones.
C. The Stradivarius violin, because of the unique wood and finish used in its construction, is widely regarded as the finest string instrument ever manufactured in the world.
D. A close study of the Stradivarius violin has revealed that the best wood for making violins is Venetian spruce, stored underwater.

21. People who watch the display of fireflies on a clear summer evening are actually witnessing a complex chemical reaction called "bioluminescence," which turns certain organisms into living light bulbs. Organisms that produce this light undergo a reaction in which oxygen combines with a chemical called lucerfin and an enzyme called luciferase. Depending on the organism, the light produced from this reaction can range from the light green of the firefly to the bright red spots of a railroad worm. 21.____

A. Although the function of most displays of bioluminescence is to attract mates, as is the case with fireflies, other species rely on bioluminescence for different purposes.

B. Bioluminescence, a phenomenon produced by several organisms, is the result of a chemical reaction that takes place within the body of the organism.
C. Of all the organisms in the world, only insects are capable of displaying bioluminescence.
D. Despite the fact that some organisms display bioluminescence, these reactions produce almost no heat, which is why the light they create is sometimes referred to as cold light.

22. The first of America's "log cabin" presidents, Andrew Jackson rose from humble backcountry origins to become a U.S. congressman and senator, a renowned military hero, and the seventh president of the United States. Among many Americans, especially those of the western frontier, he was acclaimed as a symbol of the "new" American: self-made, strong through closeness to nature, and endowed with a powerful moral courage. 22.____
A. Andrew Jackson was the first American president to rise from modest origins.
B. Because he was born poor, President Andrew Jackson was more popular among Americans of the western frontier.
C. Andrew Jackson's humble background, along with his outstanding achievements, made him into a symbol of American strength and self-sufficiency.
D. Andrew Jackson achieved success as a legislator, soldier, and president because he was born humbly and had to work for every honor he ever received.

23. In the past few decades, while much of the world's imagination has focused on the possibilities of outer space, some scientists have been exploring a different frontier—the ocean floor. Although ships have been sailing the oceans for centuries, only recently have scientists developed vehicles strong enough to sustain the pressure of deep-sea exploration and observation. These fiberglass vehicles, called submersibles, are usually just big enough to take two or three people to the deepest parts of the oceans' floors. 23.____
A. Modern submersible vehicles, thanks to recent technological innovations, are now exploring underwater cliffs, crevices, and mountain ranges that were once unreachable.
B. While most people tend to fantasize about exploring outer space, they should be turning toward a more accessible realm—the depths of the earth's oceans.
C. Because of the necessarily small size of submersible vehicles, exploration of the deep ocean is not a widespread activity.
D. Recent technological developments have helped scientists to turn their attention from deep space to the deep ocean.

24. The panda—a native of the remote mountainous regions of China—subsists almost entirely on the tender shoots of the bamboo plant. This restrictive diet has allowed the panda to evolve an anatomical structure that is completely different from that of other bears, whose paws are aligned for running, stabbing, and scratching. The panda's paw has an over-developed wrist bone that juts out below the other claws like a thumb, and the panda uses this "thumb" to grip bamboo shoots while it strips them of their leaves. 24.____
   A. The panda is the only bear-like animal that feeds on vegetation, and it has a kind of thumb to help it grip bamboo shoots.
   B. The panda's limited diet of bamboo has led it to evolve a thumb-like appendage for grasping bamboo shoots.
   C. The panda's thumb-like appendage is a factor that limits its diet to the shoots of the bamboo plant.
   D. Because bamboo shoots must be held tightly while eaten, the panda's thumb-like appendage ensure that it is the only bear-like animal that eats bamboo.

25. The stability and security of the Balkan region remains a primary concern for Greece in post-Cold War Europe, and Greece's active participation in peacekeeping and humanitarian operations in Georgia, Albania, and Bosnia are substantial examples of this commitment. Due to its geopolitical position, Greece believes it necessary to maintain, at least for now, a more nationalized defense force than other European nations. It is Greece's hope that the new spirit of integration and cooperation will help establish a common European foreign affairs and defense policy that might ease some of these regional tensions, and allow a greater level of Greek participation in NATO's integrated military structure. 25.____
   A. Greece's proximity to the unstable Balkan region has led it to keep a more nationalized military, though it hopes to become more involved in a common European defense force.
   B. The Balkan states present a greater threat to Greece than any other European nation, and Greece has adopted a highly nationalist military force as a result.
   C. Greece, the only Balkan state to belong to NATO, has an isolationist approach to defense, but hopes to achieve greater integration in the organization's combined forces.
   D. Greece's failure to become more militarily integrated with the rest of Europe can be attributed to the failure to establish a common European defense policy.

KEY (CORRECT ANSWERS)

1.	A	11.	A
2.	B	12.	D
3.	B	13.	C
4.	D	14.	B
5.	C	15.	D
6.	B	16.	D
7.	C	17.	B
8.	D	18.	A
9.	C	19.	C
10.	D	20.	A

21.	B
22.	C
23.	D
24.	B
25.	A

PREPARING WRITTEN MATERIAL

PARAGRAPH REARRANGEMENT COMMENTARY

The sentences that follow are in scrambled order. You are to rearrange them in proper order and indicate the letter choice containing the correct answer at the space at the right.

Each group of sentences in this section is actually a paragraph presented in scrambled order. Each sentence in the group has a place in that paragraph; no sentence is to be left out. You are to read each group of sentences and decide upon the best order in which to put the sentences so as to form a well-organized paragraph.

The questions in this section measure the ability to solve a problem when all the facts relevant to its solution are not given.

More specifically, certain positions of responsibility and authority require the employee to discover connection between events sometimes, apparently, unrelated. In order to do this, the employee will find it necessary to correctly infer that unspecified events have probably occurred or are likely to occur. This ability becomes especially important when action must be taken on incomplete information.

Accordingly, these questions require competitors to choose among several suggested alternatives, each of which presents a different sequential arrangement of the events. Competitors must choose the MOST logical of the suggested sequences.

In order to do so, they may be required to draw on general knowledge to infer missing concepts or events that are essential to sequencing the given events. Competitors should be careful to infer only what is essential to the sequence. The plausibility of the wrong alternatives will always require the inclusion of unlikely events or of additional chains of events which are NOT essential to sequencing the given events.

It's very important to remember that you are looking for the best of the four possible choices, and that the best choice of all may not even be one of the answers you're given to choose from.

There is no one right way to solve these problems. Many people have found it helpful to first write out the order of the sentences, as they would have arranged them, on their scrap paper before looking at the possible answers. If their optimum answer is there, this can save them some time. If it isn't, this method can still give insight into solving the problem. Others find it most helpful to just go through each of the possible choices, contrasting each as they go along. You should use whatever method feels comfortable and works for you.

While most of these types of questions are not that difficult, we've added a higher percentage of the difficult type, just to give you more practice. Usually there are only one or two questions on this section that contain such subtle distinctions that you're unable to answer confidently. And you then may find yourself stuck deciding between two possible choices, neither of which you're sure about.

EXAMINATION SECTION

TEST 1

DIRECTIONS: The following groups of sentences need to be arranged in an order that makes sense. Select the letter preceding the sequence that represents the BEST sentence order. *PRINT THE LETTER OF THE CORRECT ANSWER IN THE SPACE AT THE RIGHT.*

1. I. The keyboard was purposely designed to be a little awkward to slow typists down. 1.____
   II. The arrangement of letters on the keyboard of a typewriter was not designed for the convenience of the typist.
   III. Fortunately, no one is suggesting that a new keyboard be designed right away.
   IV. If one were, we would have to learn to type all over again.
   V. The reason was that the early machines were slower than the typists and would jam easily.

   The CORRECT answer is:
   A. I, III, IV, II, V
   B. II, V, I, IV, III
   C. V, I, II, III, IV
   D. II, I, V, III, IV

2. I. The majority of the new service jobs are part-time or low-paying. 2.____
   II. According to the U.S. Bureau of Labor Statistics, jobs in the service sector constitute 72% of all jobs in this country.
   III. If more and more workers receive less and less money, who will buy the goods and services needed to keep the economy going?
   IV. The service sector is by far the fastest growing part of the United States economy.
   V. Some economists look upon this trend with great concern.

   The CORRECT answer is:
   A. II, IV, I, V, III
   B. II, III, IV, I, V
   C. V, IV, II, III, I
   D. III, I, II, IV, V

3. I. They can also affect one's endurance. 3.____
   II. This can stabilize blood sugar levels, and ensure that the brain is receiving a steady, constant, supply of glucose, so that one is *hitting on all cylinders* while taking the test.
   III. By food, we mean real food, not junk food or unhealthy snacks.
   IV. For this reason, it is important not to skip a meal, and to bring food with you to the exam.
   V. One's blood sugar levels can affect how clearly one is able to think and concentrate during an exam.

   The CORRECT answer is:
   A. V, IV, II, III, I
   B. V, II, I, IV, III
   C. V, I, IV, III, II
   D. V, IV, I, III, II

4. I. Those who are the embodiment of desire are absorbed in material quests, and those who are the embodiment of feeling are warriors who value power more than possession. 4.____
   II. These qualities are in everyone, but in different degrees.
   III. But those who value understanding yearn not for goods or victory, but for knowledge.
   IV. According to Plato, human behavior flows from three main sources: desire, emotion, and knowledge.
   V. In the perfect state, the industrial forces would produce but not rule, the military would protect but not rule, and the forces of knowledge, the philosopher kings, would reign.

   The CORRECT answer is:
   A. IV, V, I, II, III
   B. V, I, II, III, IV
   C. IV, III, II, I, V
   D. IV, II, I, III, V

5. I. Of the more than 26,000 tons of garbage produced daily in New York City, 12,000 tons arrive daily at Fresh Kills. 5.____
   II. In a month, enough garbage accumulates there to fill the Empire State Building.
   III. In 1937, the Supreme Court halted the practice of dumping the trash of New York City into the sea.
   IV. Although the garbage is compacted, in a few years the mounds of garbage at Fresh Kills will be the highest points south of Maine's Mount Desert Island on the Eastern Seaboard.
   V. Instead, tugboats now pull barges of much of the trash to Staten Island and the largest landfill in the world, Fresh Kills.

   The CORRECT answer is:
   A. III, V, IV, I, II
   B. III, V, II, IV, I
   C. III, V, I, II, IV
   D. III, II, V, IV, I

6. I. Communists rank equality very high, but freedom very low. 6.____
   II. Unlike communists, conservatives place a high value on freedom and a very low value on equality.
   III. A recent study demonstrated that one way to classify people's political beliefs is to look at the importance placed on two words: freedom and equality.
   IV. Thus, by demonstrating how members of these groups feel about the two words, the study has proved to be useful for political analysts in several European countries.
   V. According to the study, socialists and liberals rank both freedom and equality very high, while fascists rate both very low.

   The CORRECT answer is:
   A. III, V, I, II, IV
   B. V, IV, III, I, II
   C. III, V, IV, II, I
   D. III, I, II, IV, V

7. I. "Can there be anything more amazing than this?" 7.____
II. If the riddle is successfully answered, his dead brothers will be brought back to life.
III. "Even though man sees those around him dying every day," says Dharmaraj, "he still believes and acts as if he were immortal."
IV. "What is the cause of ceaseless wonder?" asks the Lord of the Lake.
V. In the ancient epic, The Mahabharata, a riddle is asked of one of the Pandava brothers.
The CORRECT answer is:
A. V, II, I, IV, III
B. V, IV, III, I, II
C. V, II, IV, III, I
D. V, II, IV, I, III

8. I. On the contrary, the two main theories—the cooperative (neoclassical) theory and the radical (labor theory)—clearly rest on very different assumptions, which have very different ethical overtones. 8.____
II. The distribution of income is the primary factor in determining the relative levels of material well-being that different groups or individuals attain.
III. Of all issues in economics, the distribution of income is one of the most controversial.
IV. The neoclassical theory tends to support the existing income distribution (or minor changes), while the labor theory ends to support substantial changes in the way income is distributed.
V. The intensity of the controversy reflects the fact that different economic theories are not purely neutral, *detached* theories with no ethical or moral implications.
The CORRECT answer is:
A. II, I, V, IV, III
B. III, II, V, I, IV
C. III, V, II, I, IV
D. III, V, IV, I, II

9. I. The pool acts as a broker and ensures that the cheapest power gets used first. 9.____
II. Every six seconds, the pool's computer monitors all of the generating stations in the state and decides which to ask for more power and which to cut back.
III. The buying and selling of electrical power is handled by the New York Power Pool in Guilderland, New York.
IV. This is to the advantage of both the buying and selling utilities.
V. The pool began operation in 1970, and consists of the state's eight electric utilities.
The CORRECT answer is:
A. V, I, II, III, IV
B. IV, II, I, III, V
C. III, V, I, IV, II
D. V, III, IV, II, I

10. I. Modern English is much simpler grammatically than Old English. 10.____
II. Finnish grammar is very complicated; there are some fifteen cases, for example.
III. Chinese, a very old language, may seem to be the exception, but it is the great number of characters/words that must be mastered that makes it so difficult to learn, not its grammar.
IV. The newest literary language—that is, written as well as spoken—is Finish, whose literary roots go back only to about the middle of the nineteenth century.
V. Contrary to popular belief, the longer a language is been in use the simpler its grammar—not the reverse.

The CORRECT answer is:
A. IV, I, II, III, V
B. V, I, IV, II, III
C. I, II, IV, III, V
D. IV, II, III, I, V

KEY (CORRECT ANSWERS)

1.	D	6.	A
2.	A	7.	C
3.	C	8.	B
4.	D	9.	C
5.	C	10.	B

TEST 2

DIRECTIONS: This type of question tests your ability to recognize accurate paraphrasing, well-constructed paragraphs, and appropriate style and tone. It is important that the answer you select contains only the facts or concepts given in the original sentences. It is also important that you be aware of incomplete sentences, inappropriate transitions, unsupported opinions, incorrect usage, and illogical sentence order. Paragraphs that do not include all the necessary facts and concepts, that distort them, or that add new ones are not considered correct.

The format for this section may vary. Sometimes, long paragraphs are given, and emphasis is placed on style and organization. Our first five questions are of this type. Other times, the paragraphs are shorter, and there is less emphasis on style and more emphasis on accurate representation of information. Our second group of five questions are of this nature.

For each of Questions 1 through 10, select the paragraph that BEST expresses the ideas contained in the sentences above it. *PRINT THE LETTER OF THE CORRECT ANSWER IN THE SPACE AT THE RIGHT.*

1. I. Listening skills are very important for managers. 1.____
   II. Listening skills are not usually emphasized.
   III. Whenever managers are depicted in books, manuals or the media, they are always talking, never listening.
   IV. We'd like you to read the enclosed handout on listening skills and to try to consciously apply them this week.
   V. We guarantee they will improve the quality of your interactions.

   A. Unfortunately, listening skills are not usually emphasized for managers. Managers are always depicted as talking, never listening. We'd like you to read the enclosed handout on listening skills. Please try to apply these principles this week. If you do, we guarantee they will improve the quality of your interactions.
   B. The enclosed handout on listening skills will be important improving the quality of your interactions. We guarantee it. All you have to do is take sometime this week to read and to consciously try to apply the principles. Listening skills are very important for manages, but they are not usually emphasized. Whenever managers are depicted in books, manuals or the media, they are always talking, never listening.
   C. Listening well is one of the most important skills a manager can have, yet it's not usually given much attention. Think about any representation of managers in books, manuals, or in the media that you may have seen. They're always talking, never listening. We'd like you to read the enclosed handout on listening skills and consciously try to apply them the rest of the week. We guarantee you will see a difference in the quality of your interactions.

D. Effective listening, one very important tool in the effective manager's arsenal, is usually not emphasized enough. The usual depiction of managers in books, manuals or the media is one in which they are always talking, never listening. We'd like you to read the enclosed handout and consciously try to apply the information contained therein throughout the rest of the week. We feel sure that you will see a marked difference in the quality of your interactions.

2. I. Chekhov wrote three dramatic masterpieces which share certain themes and formats: Uncle Vanya, The Cherry Orchard, and The Three Sisters. 2.____
II. They are primarily concerned with the passage of time and how this erodes human aspirations.
III. The plays are haunted by the ghosts of the wasted life.
IV. The characters are concerned with life's lesser problems; however, such as the inability to make decisions, loyalty to the wrong cause, and the inability to be clear.
V. This results in sweet, almost aching, type of a sadness referred to as Chekhovian.

A. Chekhov wrote three dramatic masterpieces: Uncle Vanya, The Cherry Orchard, and The Three Sisters. These masterpieces share certain themes and formats: the passage of time, how time erodes human aspirations, and the ghosts of wasted life. Each masterpiece is characterized by a sweet, almost aching, type of sadness that has become known as Chekhovian. The sweetness of this sadness hinges on the fact that it is not the great tragedies of life which are destroying these characters, but their minor flaws: indecisiveness, misplaced loyalty, unclarity.
B. The Cherry Orchard, Uncle Vanya, and The Three Sisters are three dramatic masterpieces written by Chekhov that use similar formats to explore a common theme. Each is primarily concerned with the way that passing time wears down human aspirations, and each is haunted by the ghosts of the wasted life. The characters are shown struggling futilely with the lesser problems of life: indecisiveness, loyalty to the wrong cause, and the inability to be clear. These struggles create a mood of sweet, almost aching, sadness that has become known as Chekhovian.
C. Chekhov's dramatic masterpieces are, along with The Cherry Orchard, Uncle Vanya, and The Three Sisters. These plays share certain thematic and formal similarities. They are concerned most of all with the passage of time and the way in which time erodes human aspirations. Each play is haunted by the specter of the wasted life. Chekhov's characters are caught, however, by life's lesser snares: indecisiveness, loyalty to the wrong cause, and unclarity. The characteristic mood is a sweet, almost aching type of sadness that has come to be known as Chekhovian.
D. A Chekhovian mood is characterized by sweet, almost aching, sadness. The term comes from three dramatic tragedies by Chekhov which revolve around the sadness of a wasted life. The three masterpieces (Uncle Vanya, The Three Sisters, and The Cherry Orchard) share the same

theme and format. The plays are concerned with how the passage of time erodes human aspirations. They are peopled with characters who are struggling with life's lesser problems. These are people who are indecisive, loyal to the wrong causes, or are unable to make themselves clear.

3. I. Movie previews have often helped producers decide which parts of movies they should take out or leave in. 3.____
   II. The first 1933 preview of King Kong was very helpful to the producers because many people ran screaming from the theater and would not return when four men first attacked by Kong were eaten by giant spiders.
   III. The 1950 premiere of Sunset Boulevard resulted in the filming of an entirely new beginning, and a delay of six months in the film's release.
   IV. In the original opening scene, William Holden was in a morgue talking with thirty-six other "corpses" about the ways some of them had died.
   V. When he began to tell them of his life with Gloria Swanson, the audience found this hilarious, instead of taking the scene seriously.

   A. Movie previews have often helped producers decide what parts of movies they should leave in or take out. For example, the first preview of King Kong in 1933 was very helpful. In one scene, four men were first attacked by Kong and then eaten by giant spiders. Many members of the audience ran screaming from the theater and would not return. The premiere of the 1950 film Sunset Boulevard was also very helpful. In the original opening scene, William Holden was in a morgue with thirty-six other "corpses," discussing the ways some of them had died. When he began to tell them of his life with Gloria Swanson, the audience found this hilarious. They were supposed to take the scene seriously. The result was a delay of six months in the release of the film while a new beginning was added.
   B. Movie previews have often helped producers decide whether they should change various parts of a movie. After the 1933 preview of King Kong, a scene in which four men who had been attacked by Kong were eaten by giant spiders was taken out as many people ran screaming from the theater and would not return. The 1950 premiere of Sunset Boulevard also led to some changes. In the original opening scene, William Holden was in a morgue talking with thirty-six other "corpses" about the ways some of them had died. When he began to tell them of his life with Gloria Swanson, the audience found this hilarious, instead of taking the scene seriously.
   C. What do Sunset Boulevard and King Kong have in common? Both show the value of using movie previews to test audience reaction. The first 1933 preview of King Kong showed that a scene showing four men being eaten by giant spiders after having been attacked by Kong was too frightening for many people. They ran screaming from the theater and couldn't be coaxed back. The 1950 premiere of Sunset Boulevard was also a scream, but not the kind the producers intended. The movie opens

with William Holden lying in a morgue discussing the ways they had died with thirty-six other "corpses." When he began to tell them of his life with Gloria Swanson, the audience couldn't take him seriously. Their laughter caused a six-month delay while the beginning was rewritten.

D. Producers very often use movie previews to decide if changes are needed. The premiere of Sunset Boulevard in 1950 led to a new beginning and a six-month delay in film release. At the beginning, William Holden and thirty-six other "corpses" discuss the ways some of them died. Rather than taking this seriously, the audience thought it was hilarious when he began to tell them of his life with Gloria Swanson. The first 1933 preview of King Kong was very helpful for its producers because one scene so terrified the audience that many of them ran screaming from the theater and would not return. In this particular scene, four men who had first been attacked by Kong were eaten by giant spiders.

4. I. It is common for supervisors to view employees as "things" to be manipulated. 4.____

II. This approach does not motivate employees, nor does the carrot-and-stick approach because employees often recognize these behaviors and resent them.

III. Supervisors can change these behaviors by using self-inquiry and persistence.

IV. The best managers genuinely respect those they work with, are supportive and helpful, and are interested in working as a team with those they supervise.

V. They disagree with the Golden Rule that says "he or she who has the gold makes the rules."

A. Some managers act as if they think the Golden Rule means "he or she who has the gold makes the rules." They show disrespect to employees by seeing them as "things" to be manipulated. Obviously, this approach does not motivate employees any more than the carrot-and-stick approach motivates them. The employees are smart enough to spot these behaviors and resent them. On the other hand, the managers genuinely respect those they work with, are supportive and helpful, and are interested in working as a team. Self-inquiry and persistence can change even the former type of supervisor into the latter.

B. Many supervisors all into the trap of viewing employees as "things" to be manipulated, or try to motivate them by using a carrot-and-stick approach. These methods do not motivate employees, who often recognize the behaviors and resent them. Supervisors can change these behaviors, however, by using self-inquiry and persistence. The best managers are supportive and helpful, and have genuine respect for those with whom they work. They are interested in working as a team with those they supervise. To them, the Golden Rule is not "he or she who has the gold makes the rules."

C. Some supervisors see employees as "things" to be used or manipulated using a carrot-and-stick technique. These methods don't work. Employees often see through them and resent them. A supervisor who wants to change may do so. The techniques of self-inquiry and persistence can be used to turn him or her into the type of supervisor who doesn't think the Golden Rule is "he or she who has the gold makes the rules." They may become like the best managers who treat those with whom they work with respect and give them help and support. These are the manager who know how to build a team.

D. Unfortunately, many supervisors act as if their employees are objects whose movements they can position at will. This mistaken belief has the same result as another popular motivational technique—the carrot-and-stick approach. Both attitudes can lead to the same result—resentment from those employees who recognize the behaviors for what they are. Supervisors who recognize these behaviors can change through the use of persistence and the use of self-inquiry. It's important to remember that the best managers respect their employees. They readily give necessary help and support and are interested in working as a team with those they supervise. To these managers, the Golden Rule is not "he or she who has the gold makes the rules."

5. I. The first half of the nineteenth century produced a group of pessimistic poets—Byron, De Musset, Heine, Pushkin, and Leopardi. 5.____
II. It also produced a group of pessimistic composers—Schubert, Chopin, Schumann, and even the later Beethoven.
III. Above all, in philosophy, there was the profoundly pessimistic philosopher, Schopenhauer.
IV. The Revolution was dead, the Bourbons were restored, the feudal barons were reclaiming their land, and progress everywhere was being suppressed, as the great age was over.
V. "I thank God," said Goethe, "that I am not young in so thoroughly finished a world."

A. "I thank God," said Goethe, "that I am not young in so thoroughly finished a world." The Revolution was dead, the Bourbons were restored, the feudal barons were reclaiming their land, and progress everywhere was being suppressed. The first half of the nineteenth century produced a group of pessimistic poets: Byron, De Musset, Heine, Pushkin, and Leopardi. It also produced pessimistic composers: Schubert, Chopin, Schumann. Although Beethoven came later, he fits into this group, too. Finally and above all, it also produced a profoundly pessimistic philosopher, Schopenhauer. The great age was over.

B. The first half of the nineteenth century produced a group of pessimistic poets: Byron, De Musset, Heine, Pushkin, and Leopardi. It produced a group of pessimistic composers: Schubert, Chopin, Schumann, and even the later Beethoven. Above all, it produced a profoundly pessimistic philosopher, Schopenhauer. For each of these men, the great age was over. The Revolution was dead, and the Bourbons were restored. The feudal barons were reclaiming their land, and progress everywhere was being suppressed.

C. The great age was over. The Revolution was dead—the Bourbons were restored, and the feudal barons were reclaiming their land. Progress everywhere was being suppressed. Out of this climate came a profound pessimism. Poets, like Byron, De Musset, Heine, Pushkin, and Leopardi; composers, like Schubert, Chopin, Schumann, and even the later Beethoven; and above all, a profoundly pessimistic philosopher, Schopenauer. This pessimism which arose in the first half of the nineteenth century is illustrated by these words of Goethe, "I thank God that I am not young in so thoroughly finished a world."

D. The first half of the nineteenth century produced a group of pessimistic poets, Byron, De Musset, Heine, Pushkin, and Leopardi—and a group of pessimistic composers, Schubert, Chopin, Schumann, and the later Beethoven. Above it all, it produced a profoundly pessimistic philosopher, Schopenhauer. The great age was over. The Revolution was dead, the Bourbons were restored, the feudal barons were reclaiming their land, and progress everywhere was being suppressed. "I thank God," said Goethe, "that I am not young in so thoroughly finished a world."

6. I. A new manager sometimes may feel insecure about his or her competence in the new position. 6.____

II. The new manager may then exhibit defensive or arrogant behavior towards those one supervises, or the new manager may direct overly flattering behavior toward one's new supervisor.

A. Sometimes, a new manager may feel insecure about his or her ability to perform well in this new position. The insecurity may lead him or her to treat others differently. He or she may display arrogant or defensive behavior towards those he or she supervises, or be overly flattering to his or her new supervisor.

B. A new manager may sometimes feel insecure about his or her ability to perform well in the new position. He or she may then become arrogant, defensive, or overly flattering towards those he or she works with.

C. There are times when a new manager may be insecure about how well he or she can perform in the new job. The new manager may also behave defensive or act in an arrogant way towards those he or she supervises, or overly flatter his or her boss.

D. Sometimes a new manager may feel insecure about his or her ability to perform well in the new position. He or she may then display arrogant or defensive behavior towards those they supervise, or become overly flattering towards their supervisors.

7. I. It is possible to eliminate unwanted behavior by bringing it under stimulus control—tying the behavior to a cue, and then never, or rarely, giving the cue. 7.____

II. One trainer successfully used this method to keep an energetic young porpoise from coming out of her tank whenever she felt like it, which was potentially dangerous.

III. Her trainer taught her to do it for a reward, in response to a hand signal, and then rarely gave the signal.

A. Unwanted behavior can be eliminated by tying the behavior to a cue, and then never, or rarely, giving the cue. This is called stimulus control. One trainer was able to use this method to keep an energetic young porpoise from coming out of her tank by teaching her to come out for a reward in response to a hand signal, and then rarely giving the signal.
B. Stimulus control can be used to eliminate unwanted behavior. In this method, behavior is tied to a cue, and then the cue is rarely, if ever, given. One trainer was able to successfully use stimulus control to keep an energetic young porpoise from coming out of her tank whenever she felt like it—a potentially dangerous practice. She taught the porpoise to come out for a reward when she gave a hand signal, and then rarely gave the signal.
C. It is possible to eliminate behavior that is undesirable by bringing it under stimulus control by tying behavior to a signal, and then rarely giving the signal. One trainer successfully used this method to keep an energetic porpoise from coming out of her tank, a potentially dangerous situation. Her trainer taught the porpoise to do it for a reward, in response to a hand signal, and then would rarely give the signal.
D. By using stimulus control, it is possible to eliminate unwanted behavior by tying the behavior to a cue, and then rarely or never give the cue. One trainer was able to use this method to successfully stop a young porpoise from coming out of her tank whenever she felt like it. To curb this potentially dangerous practice, the porpoise was taught by the trainer to come out of the tank for a reward, in response to a hand signal, and then rarely given the signal.

8. I. There is a great deal of concern over the safety of commercial trucks, caused by their greatly increased role in serious accidents since federal deregulation in 1981. 8.____
II. Recently, 60 percent of trucks in New York and Connecticut and 70 percent of trucks in Maryland randomly stopped by state troopers failed safety inspections.
III. Sixteen states in the United States require no training at all for truck drivers.

A. Since federal deregulation in 1981, there has been a great deal of concern over the safety of commercial trucks, and their greatly increased role in serious accidents. Recently, 60 percent of trucks in New York and Connecticut, and 70 percent of trucks in Maryland failed safety inspections. Sixteen states in the United States require no training at all for truck drivers.
B. There is a great deal of concern over the safety of commercial trucks since federal deregulation in 1981. Their role in serious accidents has greatly increased. Recently, 60 percent of trucks randomly stopped in Connecticut and New York and 70 percent in Maryland failed safety inspections conducted by state troopers. Sixteen states in the United States provide no training at all for truck drivers.
C. Commercial trucks have a greatly increased role in serious accidents since federal deregulation in 1981. This has led to a great deal of concern.

Recently, 70 percent of trucks in Maryland and 60 percent of trucks in New York and Connecticut failed inspection of those that were randomly stopped by state troopers. Sixteen states in the United States require no training for all truck drivers.

D. Since federal deregulation in 1981, the role that commercial trucks have played in serious accidents has greatly increased, and this has led to a great deal of concern. Recently, 60 percent of trucks in New York and Connecticut, and 70 percent of trucks in Maryland randomly stopped by state troopers failed safety inspections. Sixteen states in the U.S. don't require any training for truck drivers.

9. I. No matter how much some people have, they still feel unsatisfied and want more, or want to keep what they have forever. 9.____

II. One recent television documentary showed several people flying from New York to Paris for a one-day shopping spree to buy platinum earrings, because they were bored.

III. In Brazil, some people were ordering coffins that cost a minimum of $45,000 and are equipping them with deluxe stereos, televisions, and other graveyard necessities.

A. Some people, despite having a great deal, still feel unsatisfied and want more, or think they can keep what they have forever. One recent documentary on television showed several people enroute from Paris to New York for a one day shopping spree to buy platinum earrings, because they were bored. Some people in Brazil are even ordering coffins equipped with such graveyard necessities as deluxe stereos and televisions. The price of the coffins start at $45,000.

B. No matter how much some people have, they may feel unsatisfied. This leads them to want more, or to want to keep what they have forever. Recently, a television documentary depicting several people flying from New York to Paris for a one day shopping spree to buy platinum earrings. They were bored. Some people in Brazil are ordering coffins that cost at least $45,000 and come equipped with deluxe televisions, stereos and other necessary graveyard items.

C. Some people will be dissatisfied no matter how much they have. They may want more, or they may want to keep what they have forever. One recent television documentary showed several people, motivated by boredom, jetting from New York to Paris for a one-day shopping spree to buy platinum earrings. In Brazil, some people are ordering coffins equipped with deluxe stereos, televisions and other graveyard necessities. The minimum price for these coffins—$45,000.

D. Some people are never satisfied. No matter how much they have they still want more, or think they can keep what they have forever. One television documentary recently showed several people flying from New York to Paris for the day to buy platinum earrings because they were bored. In Brazil, some people are ordering coffins that cost $45,000 and are equipped with deluxe stereos, televisions and other graveyard necessities.

10. I. A television signal or video signal has three parts. 10.____
II. Its parts are the black-and-white portion, the color portion, and the synchronizing (sync) pulses, which keep the picture stable.
III. Each video source, whether it's a camera or a video-cassette recorder contains its own generator of these synchronizing pulses to accompany the picture that it's sending in order to keep it steady and straight.
IV. In order to produce a clean recording, a video-cassette recorder must "lock-up" to the sync pulses that are part of the video it is trying to record, and this effort may be very noticeable if the device does not have gunlock.

A. There are three parts to a television or video signal: the black-and-white part, the color part, and the synchronizing (sync) pulses, which keep the picture stable. Whether it's a video-cassette recorder or a camera, each video source contains its own pulse that synchronizes and generates the picture it's sending in order to keep it straight and steady. A video-cassette recorder must "lock up" to the sync pulses that are part of the video it's trying to record. If the device doesn't have gunlock, this effort must be very noticeable.
B. A video signal or television is comprised of three parts: the black-and-white portion, the color portion, and the sync (synchronizing) pulses, which keep the picture stable. Whether it's a camera or a video-cassette recorder, each video source contains its own generator of these synchronizing pulses. These accompany the picture that it's sending in order to keep it straight and steady. A video-cassette recorder must "lock up" to the sync pulses that are part of the video it is trying to record in order to produce a clean recording. This effort may be very noticeable if the device does not have gunlock.
C. There are three parts to a television or video signal: the color portion, the black-and-white portion, and the sync (synchronizing pulses). These keep the picture stable. Each video source, whether it's a video-cassette recorder or a camera, generates these synchronizing pulses accompanying the picture it's sending in order to keep it straight and steady. If a clean recording is to be produced, a video-cassette recorder must store the sync pulses that are part of the video it is trying to record. This effort may not be noticeable if the device does not have gunlock.
D. A television signal or video signal has three parts: the black-and-white portion, the color portion, and the synchronizing (sync) pulses. It's the sync pulses which keep the picture stable, which accompany it and keep it steady and straight. Whether it's a camera or a video-cassette recorder, each video source contains its own generator of these synchronizing pulses. To produce a clean recording, a video-cassette recorder must "lock up" to the sync pulses that are part of the video it is trying to record. If the device does not have gunlock, this effort may be very noticeable.

KEY (CORRECT ANSWERS)

1.	C	6.	A
2.	B	7.	B
3.	A	8.	D
4.	B	9.	C
5.	D	10.	D

BASIC FUNDAMENTALS OF A FINANCIAL STATEMENT

TABLE OF CONTENTS

BASIC FUNDAMENTALS OF A FINANCIAL STATEMENT

COMMENTARY

The ability to read and understand a financial statement is a basic requirement for the accountant, auditor, account clerk, bookkeeper, bank examiner, budget examiner, and, of course, for the executive who must manage and administer departmental affairs.

FINANCIAL REPORTS

Are financial reports really as difficult as all that? Well, if you know they are not so difficult because you have worked with them before, this section will be of auxiliary help for you. However, if you find financial statements a bit murky, but realize their great importance to you, we ought to get along fine together. For "mathematics," all we'll use is fourth-grade arithmetic.

Accountants, like all other professionals, have developed a specialized vocabulary. Sometimes this is helpful and sometimes plain confusing (like their practice of calling the income account, "Statement of Profit and Loss," when it is bound to be one or the other). But there are really only a score or so technical terms that you will have to get straight in mind. After that is done, the whole foggy business will begin to clear and in no time at all you'll be able to talk as wisely as the next fellow.

BALANCE SHEET

Look at the sample balance sheet printed on Page 2, and we'll have an insight into how it is put together. This particular report is neither the simplest that could be issued, nor the most complicated. It is a good average sample of the kind of report issues by an up-to-date manufacturing company.

Note particularly that the balance sheet represents the situation as it stood on one particular day, December 31, not the record of a year's operation. This balance sheet is broken into two parts on the left are shown *ASSETS* and on the right *LIABILITIES*. Under the asset column, you will find listed the value of things the company owns or are owed to the company. Under liabilities are listed the things the company owes to others, plus reserves, surplus, and the stated value of the stockholders' interest in the company.

One frequently hears the comment, "Well, I don't see what a good balance sheet is anyway, because the assets and liabilities are always the same whether the company is successful or not."

It is true that they always balance and, by itself, a balance sheet doesn't tell much until it is analyzed. Fortunately, we can make a balance sheet tell its story without too much effort–often an extremely revealing story, particularly, if we compare the records of several years.

ASSETS

The first notation on the asset side of the balance sheet is *CURRENT ASSETS* (Item 1). In general, current assets include cash and things that can be turned into cash in a hurry, or that, in the normal course of business, will be turned into cash in the reasonably near future, usually within a year.

Item 2 on our sample sheet is *CASH*. Cash is just what you would expect–bills and silver in the till and money on deposit in the bank.

UNITED STATES GOVERNMENT SECURITIES is Item 3. The general practice is to show securities listed as current assets at cost or market value, whichever is lower. The figure, for all reasonable purposes, represents the amount by which total cash could be easily increased if the company wanted to sell these securities.

The next entry is *ACCOUNTS RECEIVABLE* (Item 4). Here we find the total amount of money owed to the company by its regular business creditors and collectable within the next year. Most of the money is owed to the company by its customers for goods that the company delivered on credit. If this were a department store instead of a manufacturer, what you owed the store on our charge account would be included here. Because some people fail to pay their bills, the company sets up a reserve for doubtful accounts, which it subtracts from all the money owed.

THE ABC MANUFACTURING COMPANY, INC.
CONSOLIDATED BALANCE SHEET – DECEMBER 31

Item			Item		
1. CURRENT ASSETS			16. CURRENT LIABILITIES		
2. Cash			17. Accts. Payable		$300,000
3. U.S. Government Securities			18. Accrued Taxes		800,000
4. Accounts Receivable		2,000,000	19. Accrued Wages, interest		
(less reserves)			and Other Expenses		370,000
5. Inventories (at lower of cost or			20. Total Current Liabilities		$1,470,000
market)		2,000,000	21. FIRST MORTGAGE SINK-		
6. Total Current Assets		$7,000,000	ING FUND BONDS, 3½ %		
7. INVESTMENT IN AFFILIATED			DUE 2020		$2,000,000
COMPANY			22. RESERVE FOR		
Not consolidated (at cost, not in			CONTINGENCIES		200,000
excess of net assets)		200,000	23. CAPITAL STOCK:		
8. OTHER INVESTMENTS			24. 5% Preferred Stock		
At cost, less than market		100,000	(authorized and issued		
9. PLANT IMPROVEMENT FUND		550,000	10,000 shares of $100 par		
10. PROPERTY, PLANT AND			shares of $100		
EQUIPMENT:			(par value)	$1,000,000	
Cost	$8,000,000		25. Common stock		
11. Less Reserve			(authorized and issued		
for Depreciation	5,000,000		400,000 shares of no		
12. NET PROPERTY		3,000,000	par value)	1,000,000	
13. PREPAYMENTS		50,000	26. SURPLUS:		2,000,000
14. DEFERRED CHARGES		100,000	27. Earned	3,530,000	
15. PATENTS AND GOODWILL		100,000	28. Capital (arising from sale		
			of common capital stock		
			at price in excess of		
			stated value)	1,900,000	
					5,430,000
TOTAL		$11,000,000	TOTAL		$11,100,000

Item 5, *INVENTORIES*, is the value the company places on the supplies it owns. The inventory of a manufacturer may contain raw materials that it uses in making the things it sells, partially finished goods in process of manufacture, and, finally, completed merchandise that it is ready to sell. Several methods are used to arrive at the value placed on these various items. The most common is to value them at their cost or present market value, whichever is lower.

You can be reasonably confident, however, that the figure given is an honest and significant one for the particular industry if the report is certified by a reputable firm of public accountants.

Next on the asset side is *TOTAL CURRENT ASSETS* (Item 6). This is an extremely important figure when used in connection with other items in the report, which we will come to presently. Then we will discover how to make total current assets tell their story.

INVESTMENT IN AFFILIATED COMPANY Item 7) represents the cost to our parent company of the capital stock of its subsidiary or affiliated company. A subsidiary is simply one company that is controlled by another. Most corporations that own other companies outright lump the figures in a CONSOLIDATED BALANCE SHEET. This means that, under cash, for example, one would find a total figure that represented all of the cash of the parent company and of its wholly owned subsidiary. This is a perfectly reasonable procedure because, in the last analysis, all of the money is controlled by the same persons.

Our typical company shows that it has *OTHER INVESTMENTS* (Item 8), in addition to its affiliated company. Sometimes good marketable securities other than Government bonds are carried as current assets, but the more conservative practice is to list these other security holdings separately. If they have been bought as a permanent investment, they would always be shown by themselves. "At cost, less than market" means that our company paid $100,000 for these other investments, but they are now worth more.

Among our assets is a *PLANT IMPROVEMENT FUND* (Item 9). Of course, this item does not appear in all company balance sheets, but is typical of special funds that companies set up for one purpose or another. For example, money set aside to pay off part of the bonded debt of a company might be segregated into a special fund. The money our directors have put aside to improve the plant would often be invested in Government bonds,

FIXED ASSETS

The next item (10) is *PROPERTY, PLANT, AND EQUIPMENT*, but it might just as well be labeled Fixed Assets as these items are used more or less interchangeably, Under Item 10, the report gives the value of land, buildings, and machinery and such movable things as trucks, furniture, and hand tools. Historically, probably more sins were committed against this balance sheet item than any other.

In olden days, cattlemen used to drive their stock to market in the city. It was a common trick to stop outside of town, spread out some salt for the cattle to make them thirsty and then let them drink all the water they could hold. When they were weighed for sale, the cattlemen would collect cash for the water the stock had drunk. Business buccaneers, taking the cue from their farmer friends, would often "write up" the value of their fixed assets. In other words, they would increase the value shown on the balance sheet, making the capital stock appear to be worth a lot more than it was. *Watered stock* proved a bad investment for most stockholders. The practice has, fortunately, been stopped, though it took major financial reorganizations to squeeze the water out of some securities.

The most common practice today is to list fixed assets at cost. Often, there is no ready market for most of the things that fall under this heading, so it is not possible to give market value. A good report will tell what is included under fixed assets and how it has been valued. If the value has been increased by *write-up* or decreased by *write-down*, a footnote explanation is usually given. A *write-up* might occur, for instance, if the value of real estate increased substantially. A *write-down* might follow the invention of a new machine that put an important part of the company's equipment out of date.

DEPRECIATION

Naturally, all of the fixed property of a company will wear out in time (except, of course, non-agricultural land). In recognition of this fact, companies set up a *RESERVE FOR APPRECIATION* (Item 11). If a truck costs $4,000 and is expected to last four years, it will be depreciated at the rate of $1,000 a year.

Two other items also frequently occur in connection with depreciation–*depletion* and *obsolescence*. Companies may lump depreciation, depletion, and obsolescence under a single title, or list them separately.

Depletion is a term used primarily by mining and oil companies (or any of the so-called extractive industries). Depletion means exhaust or use up. As the oil or other natural resource is used up, a reserve is set up, to compensate for the natural wealth the company no longer owns. This reserve is set up in recognition of the fact that, as the company sells its natural product, it must get back not only the cost of extracting but also the original cost of the natural resource.

Obsolescence represents the loss in value because a piece of property has gone out of date before it wore out. Airplanes are modern examples of assets that tend to get behind the times long before the parts wear out. (Women and husbands will be familiar with the speed at which ladies' hats "obsolesce.")

In our sample balance sheet we have placed the reserve for depreciation under fixed assets and then subtracted, giving us *NET PROPERTY* (Item 12), which we add into the asset column. Sometimes, companies put the reserve for depreciation in the liability column. As you can see, the effect is just the same whether it is *subtracted* from assets or *added* to liabilities.

The manufacturer, whose balance sheet we use, rents a New York showroom and pays his rent yearly, in advance. Consequently, he has listed under assets *PREPAYMENTS* (Item 13). This is listed as an asset because he has paid for the use of the showroom, but has not yet received the benefit from its use. The use is something coming to the firm in the following year and, hence, is an asset. The dollar value of this asset will decrease by one-twelfth each month during the coming year.

DEFERRED CHARGES (Item 14) represents a type of expenditure similar to prepayment. For example, our manufacturer brought out a new product last year, spending $100,000 introducing it to the market. As the benefit from this expenditure will be returned over months or even years to come, the manufacturer did not think it reasonable to charge the full expenditure against costs during the year. He has *deferred* the charges and will write them off gradually.

INTANGIBLES

The last entry in our asset column is *PATENTS AND GOODWILL* (Item 15). If our company were a young one, set up to manufacturer some new patented product, it would probably carry its patents at a substantial figure. In fact, *intangibles* of both old and new companies are often of great but generally unmeasurable worth.

Company practice varies considerably in assigning value to intangibles. Proctor & Gamble, despite the tremendous goodwill that has been built up for *Ivory Soap*, has reduced all of its intangibles to the nominal $1. Some of the big cigarette companies, on the contrary, place a high dollar value on the goodwill their brand names enjoy. Companies that spend a good deal for research and the development of new products are more inclined than others to reflect this fact in the value assigned to patents, license agreements, etc.

LIABILITIES

The liability side of the balance sheet appears a little deceptive at first glance. Several of the entries simply don't sound like liabilities by any ordinary definition of the term.

The first term on the liability side of any balance sheet is usually *CURRENT LIABILITIES* (Item 16). This is a companion to the Current Assets item across the page and includes all debts that fall due within the next year. The relation between current assets and current liabilities is one of the most revealing things to be gotten from the balance sheet, but we will go into that quite thoroughly later on.

ACCOUNTS PAYABLE (Item 17) represents the money that the company owes to its ordinary business creditors–unpaid bills for materials, supplies, insurance, and the like. Many companies itemize the money they owe in a much more detailed fashion than we have done, but, as you will see, the totals are the most interesting thing to us.

Item 18, *ACCRUED TAXES*, is the tax bill that the company estimates it still owes for the past year. We have lumped all taxes in our balance sheet, as many companies do. However, sometimes you will find each type of tax given separately. If the detailed procedure is followed, the description of the tax is usually quite sufficient to identify the separate items.

Accounts Payable was defined as the money the company owed to its regular business creditors. The company also owes, on any given day, wages to its own employees; interest to its bondholders and to banks from which it may have borrowed money; fees to its attorneys; pensions, etc. These are all totaled under *ACCRUED WAGES, INTEREST AND OTHER EXPENSES* (Item 19).

TOTAL CURRENT LIABILITIES (Item 20) is just the sum of everything that the company owed on December 31 and which must be paid sometime in the next twelve months.

It is quite clear that all of the things discussed above are liabilities. The rest of the entries on the liability side of the balance sheet, however, do not seem at first glance to be liabilities.

Our balance sheet shows that the company, on December 31, had $2,000,000 of 3½ percent First Mortgage BONDS outstanding (Item 21). Legally, the money received by a company when it sells bonds is considered a loan to the company. Therefore, it is obvious that the company owes to the bondholders an amount equal to the face value or the *call price* of the bonds it has outstanding. The call price is a figure usually larger than the face value of the bonds at which price the company can *call* the bonds in from the bondholders and pay them off before they ordinarily fall due. The date that often occurs as part of the name of a bond is the date at which the company has promised to pay off the loan from the bondholders.

RESERVES

The next heading, *RESERVE FOR CONTINGENCIES* (Item 22) sounds more like an asset than a liability. "My reserves," you might say, "are dollars in the bank, and dollars in the bank are assets.

No one would deny that you have something there. In fact, the corporation treasurer also has his reserve for contingencies balanced by either cash or some kind of unspecified investment on the asset side of the ledger. His reason for setting up a reserve on the liability side of the balance sheet is a precaution against making his financial position seem better than it is. He decided that the company might have to pay out this money during the coming year if certain things happened. If he did not set up the "reserve," his surplus would appear larger by an amount equal to his reserve.

A very large reserve for contingencies or a sharp increase in this figure from the previous year should be examined closely by the investor. Often, in the past, companies tried to hide their true earnings by transferring funds into a contingency reserve. As a reserve looks somewhat like a true liability, stockholders were confused about the real value of their securities. When a reserve is not set up for protection against some very probable loss or expenditure, it should be considered by the investor as part of surplus.

CAPITAL STOCK

Below reserves there is a major heading, *CAPITAL STOCK* (Item 23). Companies may have one type of security outstanding, or they may have a dozen. All of the issues that represent shares of ownership are capital, regardless of what they are called on the balance sheet–preferred stock, preference stock, common stock, founders' shares, capital stock, or something else.

Our typical company has one issue of 5 percent *PREFERRED STOCK* (Item 24). It is called *preferred* because those who own it have a right to dividends and assets before the *common* stockholders–that is, the holders are in a preferred position as owners. Usually, preferred stockholders do not have a voice in company affairs unless the company fails to pay them dividends at the promised rate. Their rights to dividends are almost always *cumulative.* This simply means that all past dividends must be paid before the other stockholders can receive anything. Preferred stockholders are not creditors of the company so it cannot properly be said that the company *owes* them the value of their holdings. However, in case the company decided to go out of business, preferred stockholders would have a prior claim on anything that was left in the company treasury after all of the creditors, including the bondholders, were paid off. In practice, this right does not always mean much, but it does explain why the book value of their holdings is carried as a liability.

COMMON STOCK (Item 25) is simple enough as far as definition is concerned. It represents the rights of the ordinary owner of the company. Each company has as many owners as it has stockholders. The proportion of the company that each stockholder owns is determined by the number of shares he has. However, neither the book value of a no-par common stock, nor the par value of an issue that has a given par, can be considered as representing either the original sale price, the market value, or what would be left for the stockholders if the company were liquidated.

A profitable company will seldom be dissolved. Once things have taken such a turn that dissolution appears desirable, the stated value of the stock is generally nothing but a fiction. Even if the company is profitable as a going institution, once it ceases to function even its tangible assets drop in value because there is not usually a ready market for its inventory of raw materials and semi-finished goods, or its plant and machinery.

SURPLUS

The last major heading on the liability side of the balance sheet is *SURPLUS* (Item 26). The surplus, of course, is not a liability in the popular sense at all. It represents, on our balance sheet, the difference between the stated value of our common stock and the net assets behind the stock.

Two different kinds of surplus frequently appear on company balance sheets, and our company has both kinds. The first type listed is *EARNED* surplus (Item 27). Earned surplus is roughly similar to your own savings. To the corporation, earned surplus is that part of net income which has not been paid to stockholders as dividends. It still belongs to you, but the directors have decided that it is best for the company and the stockholders to keep it in the business. The surplus may be invested in the plant just as you might invest part of your savings in your home. It may also be in cash or securities.

In addition to the earned surplus, our company also has a *CAPITAL* surplus (Item 28) of $1,900.00, which the balance sheet explains arose from selling the stock at a higher cost per share than is given as its stated value. A little arithmetic shows that the stock is carried on the books at $2.50 a share while the capital surplus amounts to $4.75 a share. From this we know that the company actually received an average of $7.25 net a share for the stock when it was sold.

WHAT DOES THE BALANCE SHEET SHOW?

Before we undertake to analyze the balance sheet figures, a word on just what an investor can expect to learn is in order. A generation or more ago, before present accounting standards had gained wide acceptance, considerable imagination went into the preparation of balance sheets. This, naturally, made the public skeptical of financial reports. Today, there is no substantial ground for skepticism. The certified public accountant, the listing requirements of the national stock exchanges, and the regulations of the Securities and Exchange Commission have, for all practical purposes, removed the grounds for doubting the good faith of financial reports.

The investor, however, is still faced with the task of determining the significance of the figures. As we have already seen, a number of items are based, to a large degree, upon estimates, while others are, of necessity, somewhat arbitrary.

NET WORKING CAPITAL

There is one very important thing that we can find from the balance sheet and accept with the full confidence that we know what we are dealing with. That is net working capital, sometimes simply called working capital.

On the asset side of our balance sheet, we have added up all of the current assets and show the total as Item 6. On the liability side, Item 20 gives the total of current liabilities. *Net working capital* or *net current assets* is the difference left after subtracting current liabilities from current assets. If you consider yourself an investor rather than a speculator, you should always insist that any company in which you invest have a comfortable amount of working capital. The ability of a company to meet its obligations with ease, expand its volume as business expands and take advantage of opportunities as they present themselves, is, to an important degree, determined by its working capital.

Probably the question in your mind is: "*Just what does 'comfortable amount*' of working capital mean?" Well, there are several methods used by analysts to judge whether a particular company has a sound working capital position. The first rough test for an industrial company is to compare the working capital figure with the current liability total. Most analysts say that minimum safety requires that net working capital at least equal current liabilities. Or, put another way, current assets should be at least twice as large as current liabilities.

There are so many different kinds of companies, however, that this test requires a great deal of modification if it is to be really helpful in analyzing companies in different industries. To help you interpret the current position of a company in which you are considering investing, the *current ratio* is more helpful than the dollar total of working capital. The current ratio is current assets divided by current liabilities.

In addition to working capital and current ratio, there are two other ways of testing the adequacy of the current position. *Net quick assets* provide a rigorous and important test of a company's ability to meet its current obligations. Net quick assets are found by taking total current assets (Item 6) and subtracting the value of inventories (Item 5). A well-fixed industrial company should show a reasonable excess of quick assets over current liabilities.

Finally, many analysts say that a good industrial company should have at least as much working capital (current assets less current liabilities) as the total book value of its bonds and preferred stock. In other words, current liabilities, bonded debt, and preferred stock *altogether* should not exceed the current assets.

INVENTORY AND INVENTORY TURNOVER

In the recent past, there has been much talk of inventories. Many commentators have said that these carry a serious danger to company earnings if management allows them to increase too much. Of course, this has always been true, but present high prices have made everyone more inventory-conscious than usual.

There are several dangers in a large inventory position. In the first place, sharp drop in price may cause serious losses; also, a large inventory may indicate that the company has accumulated a big supply of unsalable merchandise. The question still remains, however: "What do we mean by large inventory?"

As you certainly realize, an inventory is large or small only in terms of the yearly turnover and the type of business. We can discover the annual turnover of our sample company by dividing inventories (Item 5) into total annual sales (item "a" on the income account).

It is also interesting to compare the value of the inventory of a company being studied with total current assets. Again, however, there is considerable variation between different types of companies, so that the relationship becomes significant only when compared with similar companies.

NET BOOK VALUE OF SECURITIES

There is one other very important thing that can be gotten from the balance sheet, and that is the net book or equity value of the company's securities. We can calculate the net book value of each of the three types of securities our company has outstanding by a little very simple arithmetic. *Book value* means *the value at which something is carried on the books of the company.*

The full rights of the bondholders come before any of the rights of the stockholders, so, to find the net book value or net tangible assets backing up the bonds we add together the balance sheet value of the bonds, preferred stock, common stock, reserve, and surplus. This gives us a total of $9,630,000, (We would not include contingency reserve if we were reasonably sure the contingency was going to arise, but, as general reserves are often equivalent to surplus, it is, usually, best to treat the reserve just as though it were surplus.) However, part of this value represents the goodwill and patents carried at $100,000, which is not a tangible item, so, to be conservative, we subtract this amount, leaving $9,530,000 as the total net book value of the bonds. This is equivalent to $4,765 for each $1,000 bond, a generous figure. To calculate the net book value of the preferred stock, we must eliminate the face value of the bonds, and then, following the same procedure, add the value of the preferred stock, common stock, reserve, and surplus, and subtract goodwill. This gives us a total net book value for the preferred stock of $7,530 or $753 for each share of $100 par value preferred. This is also very good coverage for the preferred stock, but we must examine current earnings before becoming too enthusiastic about the value of any security.

The net book value of the common stock, while an interesting figure, is not so important as the coverage on the senior securities. In case of liquidation, there is seldom much left for the common stockholders because of the normal loss in value of company assets when they are put up for sale, as mentioned before. The book value figure, however, does give us a basis for comparison with other companies. Comparisons of net book value over a period of years also show us if the company is a soundly growing one or, on the other hand, is losing ground. Earnings, however, are our important measure of common stock values, as we will see shortly.

The net book value of the common stock is found by adding the stated value of the common stock, reserves, and surplus and then subtracting patents and goodwill. This gives us a total net book value of $6,530,000. As there are 400,000 shares of common outstanding, each share has a net book value of $16.32. You must be careful not to be misled by book value figures, particularly of common stock. Profitable companies (Coca-Cola, for example) often show a very low net book value and very substantial earnings. Railroads, on the other hand, may show a high book value for their common stock but have such low or irregular earnings that the market price of the stock is much less than its apparent book value. Banks, insurance companies, and investment trusts are exceptions to what we have said about common stock net book value. As their assets are largely liquid (i.e., cash, accounts receivable, and marketable securities), the book value of their common stock sometimes indicates its value very accurately.

PROPORTION OF BONDS, PREFERRED AND COMMON STOCK

Before investing, you will want to know the proportion of each kind of security issued by the company you are considering. A high proportion of bonds reduces the attractiveness of both the preferred and common stock, while too large an amount of preferred detracts from the value of the common.

The *bond ratio* is found by dividing the face value of the bonds (Item 21), or $2,000,000, by the total value of the bonds, preferred stock, common stock, reserve, and surplus, or $9,630,000. This shows that bonds amount to about 20 percent of the total of bonds, capital, and surplus.

The *preferred stock ratio* is found in the same way, only we divide the stated value of the preferred stock by the total of the other five items. Since we have half as much preferred stock as we have bonds, the preferred ratio is roughly 10.

Naturally, the *common stock ratio* will be the difference between 100 percent and the totals of the bonds and preferred, or 70 percent in our sample company. You will want to remember that the most valuable method of determining the common stock ratio is in combination with reserve and surplus. The surplus, as we have noted, is additional backing for the common stock and usually represents either original funds paid in to the company in excess of the stated value of the common stock (capital surplus), or undistributed earnings (earned surplus).

Most investment analysts carefully examine industrial companies that have more than about a quarter of their capitalization represented by bonds, while common stock should total at least as much as all senior securities (bonds and preferred issues). When this is not the case, companies often find it difficult to raise new capital. Banks don't like to lend them money because of the already large debt, and it is sometimes difficult to sell common stock because of all the bond interest or preferred dividends that must be paid before anything is available for the common stockholder.

Railroads and public utility companies are exceptions to most of the rules of thumb that we use in discussing The ABC Manufacturing Company, Inc. Their situation is different because of the tremendous amounts of money they have invested in their fixed assets, their small inventories and he ease with which they can collect their receivables. Senior securities of railroads and utility companies frequently amount to more than half of their capitalization, Speculators often interest themselves in companies that have a high proportion of debt or preferred stock because of the *leverage factor*. A simple illustration will show why. Let us take, for example, a company with $10,000,000 of 4 percent bonds outstanding. If the company is earning $440,000 before bond interest, there will be only $40,000 left for the common stock ($10,000,000 at 4% equals $400,000). However, an increase of only 10 percent in earnings (to $484,000) will leave $84,000 for common stock dividends, or an increase of more than 100 percent. If there is only a small common issue, the increase in earnings per share would appear very impressive.

You have probably already noticed that a decline of 10 percent in earnings would not only wipe out everything available for the common stock, but result in the company being unable to cover its full interest on its bonds without dipping into surplus. This is the great danger of so-called high leverage stocks and also illustrates the fundamental weakness of companies that have a disproportionate amount of debt or preferred stock. Investors would do well to steer clear of them. Speculators, however, will continue to be fascinated by the market opportunities they offer.

THE INCOME ACCOUNT

The fundamental soundness of a company, as shown by its balance sheet, is important to investors, but of even greater interest is the record of its operation. Its financial structure shows much of its ability to weather storms and pick up speed when times are good. It is the income record, however, that shows us how a company is actually doing and gives us our best guide to the future.

The *Consolidated Income and Earned Surplus* account of our company is stated on the next page. Follow the items given there and we will find out just how our company earned its money, what it did with its earnings, and what it all means in terms of our three classes of securities. We have used a combined income and surplus account because it is the form most frequently followed by industrial companies. However, sometimes the two statements are given separately. Also, a variety of names are used to describe this same part of the financial report. Sometimes it is called profit and loss account, sometimes *record of earnings*, and, often, simply *income account*. They are all the same thing.

The details that you will find on different income statements also vary a great deal. Some companies show only eight or ten separate items, while others will give a page or more of closely spaced entries that break down each individual type of revenue or cost. We have tried to strike a balance between extremes; give the major items that are in most income statements, omitting details that are only interesting to the expert analyst.

The most important source of revenue always makes up the first item on the income statement. In our company, it is *Net Sales* (Item "a"). If it were a railroad or a utility instead of a manufacturer, this item would be called *gross revenues*. In any case, it represents the money paid into the company by its customers. Net sales are given to show that the figure represents the amount of money actually received after allowing for discounts and returned goods.

Net sales or gross revenues, you will note, is given before any kind of miscellaneous revenue that might have been received from investments, the sale of company property, tax refunds, or the like. A well-prepared income statement is always set up this way so that the stockholder can estimate the success of the company in fulfilling its major job of selling goods or service. If this were not so, you could not tell whether the company was really losing or making money on its operations, particularly over the last few years when tax rebates and other unusual things have often had great influence on final net income figures.

The ABC Manufacturing Company, Inc.
CONSOLIDATED INCOME AND EARNED SURPLUS
For the Year Ended December 31

Item		
a. Sales		$10,000,000
b. COST OF SALES, EXPENSES AND OTHER OPERATING CHARGES:		
c. Cost of Goods Sold	$7,000,000	
d. Selling, Administrative & Gen. Expenses	500,000	
e. Depreciation	200,000	
f. Maintenance and Repairs	400,000	
g. Taxes (Other than Federal Inc. Taxes)	300,000	
h. NET PROFIT FROM OPERATIONS		8,400,000
i. OTHER INCOME:		$1,600,000
j. Royalties and Dividends	$250,000	
k. Interest	25,000	
l. TOTAL		$1,875,000
m. INTEREST CHARGES:		
n. Interest on Funded Debt	$70,000	
o. Other Interest	20,000	90,000
p. NET INCOME BEFORE PROVISION FOR FED. INCOME TAXES		$1,785,000
q. PROVISION FOR FEDERAL INCOME TAXES		678,300
r. NET INCOME		$1,106,700
s. DIVIDENDS		
t. Preferred Stock - $5.00 Per Share	$50,000	
u. Common Stock - $1.00 Per Share	400,000	
v. PROVISION FOR CONTINGENCIES	200,000	650,000
w. BALANCE CARRIED TO EARNED SURPLUS		456,700
x, EARNED SURPLUS – JANUARY 1		3,073,000
y. EARNED SURPLUS – DECEMBER 31		$3,530,000

COST OF SALES

A general heading, *Cost of Sales, Expenses, and Other Operating Charges* (Item "b") is characteristic of a manufacturing company, but a utility company or railroad would call all of these things *operating expenses.*

The most important subdivision is *Cost of Goods Sold* (Item "c"). Included under cost of goods sold are all of the expenses that go directly into the manufacture of the products the company sells—raw materials, wages, freight, power, and rent. We have lumped these expenses together, as many companies do. Sometimes, however, you will find each item listed separately. Analyzing a detailed income account is a pretty technical operation and had best be left to the expert.

We have shown separately, opposite "d," the *Selling, Administrative and General Expenses* of the past year. Unfortunately, there is little uniformity among companies in their treatment of these important non-manufacturing costs. Our figure includes the expenses of management; that is, executive salaries and clerical costs; commissions and salaries paid to salesmen; advertising expenses, and the like.

Depreciation ("e") shows us the amount that the company transferred from income during the year to the depreciation reserve that we ran across before as Item "11" on the balance sheet (Page 2). Depreciation must be charged against income unless the company is going to live on its own fat, something that no company can do for long and stay out of bankruptcy.

MAINTENANCE

Maintenance and Repairs (Item "f") represents the money spent to keep the plant in good operating order. For example, the truck that we mentioned under depreciation must be kept running day by day. The cost of new tires, recharging the battery, painting and mechanical repairs are all maintenance costs. Despite this day-to-day work on the truck, the company must still provide for the time when it wears out–hence, the reserve for depreciation.

You can readily understand from your own experience the close connection between maintenance and depreciation. If you do not take good care of your own car, you will have to buy a new one sooner than you would had you maintained it well. Corporations face the same problem with all of their equipment. If they do not do a good job of maintenance, much more will have to be set aside for depreciation to replace the abused tools and property.

Taxes are always with us. A profitable company always pays at least two types of taxes. One group of taxes are paid without regard to profits, and include real estate taxes, excise taxes, social security, and the like (Item "g"). As these payments are a direct part of the cost of doing business, they must be included before we can determine the *Net Profit From Operations* (Item "h").

Net Profit From Operations (sometimes called *gross profit*) tells us what the company made from manufacturing and selling its products. It is an interesting figure to investors because it indicates how efficiently and successfully the company operates in its primary purpose as a creator of wealth. As a glance at the income account will tell you, there are still several other items to be deducted before the stockholder can hope to get anything. You can also easily imagine that for many companies these other items may spell the difference between profit and loss. For these reasons, we use net profit from operations as an indicator of progress in manufacturing and merchandising efficiency, not as a judge of the investment quality of securities.

Miscellaneous Income not connected with the major purpose of the company is generally listed after net profit from operations. There are quite a number of ways that corporations increase their income, including interest and dividends on securities they own, fees for special services performed, royalties on patents they allow others to use, and tax refunds. Our income statement shows *Other Income* as Item "i," under which is shown income from *Royalties* and *Dividends* (Item "j"), and as a separate entry, *Interest* (Item "k") which the company received from its bond investments. The *Total* of other income (Item "l") shows us how much The ABC Manufacturing Company received from so-called *outside activities.* Corporations with diversified interests often receive tremendous amounts of other income.

INTEREST CHARGES

There is one other class of expenses that must be deducted from our income before we can determine the base on which taxes are paid, and that is *Interest Charges* (Item "m"). As our company has $2,000,000 worth of 3 ½ percent bonds outstanding, it will pay *Interest* on Funded Debt of $70,000 (Item "n"). During the year, the company also borrowed money from the bank, on which it, of course, paid interest, shown as *Other Interest* (Item "o").

Net Income Before Provision for Federal Income Taxes ("Item "p") is an interesting figure for historical comparison. It shows us how profitable the company was in all of its various operations. A comparison of this entry over a period of years will enable you to see how well the company had been doing as a business institution before the government stepped in for its share of net earnings. Federal taxes have varied so much in recent years that earnings before taxes are often a real help in judging business progress.

A few paragraphs back we mentioned that a profitable corporation pays two general types of taxes. We have already discussed those that are paid without reference to profits. *Provision for Federal Income Taxes* (Item "q") is ordinarily figured on the total income of the company after normal business expenses, and so appears on our income account below these charges. Bond interest, for example, as it is payment on a loan, is deducted beforehand. Preferred and common stock dividends, which are profits that go to owners of the company, come after all charges and taxes.

NET INCOME

After we have deducted all of our expenses and income taxes from total income, we get *Net Income* (Item "r"). Net income is the most interesting figure of all to the investor. Net income is the amount available to pay dividends on the preferred and common stock. From the balance sheet, we have learned a good deal about the company's stability and soundness of structure; from net profit from operations, we judge whether the company is improving in industrial efficiency. Net income tells us whether the securities of the company are likely to be a profitable investment.

The figure given for a single year is not nearly all of the store, however. As we have noted before, the historical record is usually more important than the figure for any given year. This is just as true of net income as any other item. So many things change from year to year that care must be taken not to draw hasty conclusions. During the war, Excess Profits Taxes had a tremendous effect on the earnings of many companies. In the next few years, carryback tax credits allowed some companies to show a net profit despite the fact that they had operated at a loss. Even net income can be a misleading figure unless one examines it carefully. A rough and easy way of judging how sound a figure it is would be to compare it with previous years.

The investor in stocks has a vital interest in *Dividends* (Item "s"). The first dividend that our company must pay is that on its *Preferred Stock* (Item "t"). Some companies will even pay preferred dividends out of earned surplus accumulated in the past if the net income is not large enough, but such a company is skating on thin ice unless the situation is most unusual.

The directors of our company decided to pay dividends totaling ($400,000 on the *Common Stock*, or $1 a share (Item "u"). As we have noted before, the amount of dividends paid is not determined by net income, but by a decision of the stockholders' representatives–the company's directors. Common dividends, just like preferred dividends, can be paid out of surplus if there is little or no net income. Sometimes companies do this if they have a long history of regular payments and don't want to spoil the record because of some special temporary situation that caused them to lose money. This occurs even less frequently and is more dangerous than paying preferred dividends out of surplus.

It is much more common, on the contrary, to plough earnings back into the business—a phrase you frequently see on the financial pages and in company reports. The directors of our typical company have decided to pay only $1 on the common stock, though net income would have permitted them to pay much more. They decided that the company should save the difference.

The next entry on our income account, *Provision for Contingencies* (Item "v") shows us where our reserve for contingencies arose. The treasurer of our typical company has put the provision for contingencies after dividends. However, you will discover, if you look at very many financial reports, that it is sometimes placed above net income.

All of the net income that was not paid out as dividends, or set aside for contingencies, is shown as *Balance Carried to Earned Surplus* (Item "w"). In other words, it is kept in the business. In previous years, the company had also earned more than it paid out so it had already accumulated by the beginning of the year an earned surplus of $3,073,000 (Item "x"). When we total the earned surplus accumulated during the year to that which the company had at the first of the year, we get the total earned surplus at the end of the year (Item "y"). You will notice that the total here is the same as that which we ran across on the balance sheet as Item 27.

Not all companies combine their income and surplus account. When they do not, you will find that *balance carried to surplus* will be the last item on the income account. The statement of consolidated surplus would appear as a third section of the corporation's financial report. A separate surplus account might be used if the company shifted funds for reserves to surplus during the year or made any other major changes in its method of treating the surplus account.

ANALYZING THE INCOME ACCOUNT

The income account, like the balance sheet, will tell us a lot more if we make a few detailed comparisons. The size of the totals on an income account doesn't mean much by itself. A company can have hundreds of millions of dollars in net sales and be a very bad investment. On the other hand, even a very modest profit in round figure may make a security attractive if there are only a small number of shares outstanding.

Before you select a company for investment, you will want to know something of its *margin of profit*, and how this figure has changed over the years. Finding the margin of profit is very simple. We just divide the net profit from operations (Item "h") by net sales (Item "a"). The figure we get (0.16) shows us that the company made a profit of 16 percent from operations. By itself, though, this is not very helpful. We can make it significant in two ways.

In the first place, we can compare it with the margin of profit in previous years, and, from this comparison, learn if the company excels other companies that do a similar type of business. If the margin of profit of our company is very low in comparison with other companies in the same field, it is an unhealthy sign. Naturally, if it is high, we have grounds to be optimistic.

Analysts also frequently use *operating ratio* for the same purpose. The operating ratio is the complement of the margin of profit. The margin of profit of our typical company is 16. The operating ratio is 84. You can find the operating ratio either by subtracting the margin of profit from 100 or dividing the total of operating costs ($8,400,000) by net sales ($10,000,000).

The margin of profit figure and the operating ratio, like all of those ratios we examined in connection with the balance sheet, give us general information about the company, help us judge its prospects for the future. All of these comparisons have significance for the long term as they tell us about the fundamental economic condition of the company. But you still have the right to ask: "Are the securities good investments for me now?"

Investors, as opposed to speculators, are primarily interested in two things. The first is safety for their capital and the second, regularity of income. They are also interested in the rate of return on their investment but, as you will see, the rate of return will be affected by the importance placed on safety and regularity. High income implies risk. Safety must be bought by accepting a lower return.

The safety of any security is determined primarily by the earnings of the company that are available to pay interest or dividends on the particular issues. Again, though, round dollar figures aren't of much help to us. What we want to know is the relationship between the total money available and the requirements for each of the securities issued by the company.

INTEREST COVERAGE

As the bonds of our company represent part of its debt, the first thing we want to know is how easily the company can pay the interest. From the income account we see that the company had total income of $1,875,000 (Item "1"). The interest charge on our bonds each year is $70,000 (3½ percent of $2,000,000–Item 21 on the balance sheet). Dividing total income by bond interest charges ($1,875,000 by $70,000) shows us that the company earned its bond interest 26 times over. Even after income taxes, bond interest was earned 17 times, a method of testing employed by conservative analysts. Before an industrial bond should be considered a safe investment, so our company has a wide margin of safety.

To calculate the *preferred dividend coverage* (i.e., the number of times preferred dividends were earned), we must use net income as our base, as Federal Income Taxes and all interest charges must be paid before anything is available for stockholders. As we have 10,000 shares of $100 par value of preferred stock which pays a dividend of 5 percent, the total dividend requirement for the preferred stock is $50,000 (Items 24 on the balance sheet and "t" on the income account).

EARNINGS PER COMMON SHARE

The buyer of common stocks is often more concerned with the earnings per share of his stock than he is with the dividend. It is usually earnings per share or, rather, prospective earnings per share, that influence stock market prices. Our income account does not show the earnings available for the common stock, so we must calculate it ourselves. It is net income less preferred dividends (Items "r"- "t"), or $1,056,700. From the balance sheet, we know that there are 400,000 shares outstanding, so the company earned about $2.64 per share.

All of these ratios have been calculated for a single year. It cannot be emphasized too strongly, however, that the record is more important to the investor than the report of any single year. By all the tests we have employed, both the bonds and the preferred stock of our typical company appear to be very good investments, if their market prices were not too high. The investor would want to look back, however, to determine whether the operations were reasonably typical of the company.

Bonds and preferred stocks that are very safe usually sell at pretty high prices, so the yield to the investor is small. For example, if our company has been showing about the same coverage on its preferred dividends for many years and there is good reason to believe that the future will be equally kind, the company would probably replace the old 5 percent preferred with a new issue paying a lower rate, perhaps 4 percent.

STOCK PRICES

As the common stock does not receive a guaranteed dividend, its market value is determined by a great variety of influences in addition to the present yield of the stock measured by its dividends. The stock market, by bringing together buyers and sellers from all over the world, reflects their composite judgment of the present and future value of the stock. We cannot attempt here to write a treatise on the stock market. There is one important ratio, however, that every common stock buyer considers. That is the ratio of earnings to market price.

The so-called *price-earnings ratio* is simply the earnings per share on the common stock divided into the market price. Our typical company earned $2.64 a common share in the year. If the stock were selling at $30 a share, its price-earnings ratio would be about 11.4. This is the basis figure that you would want to use in comparing the common stock of this particular company with other similar stocks.

IMPORTANT TERMS AND CONCEPTS

LIABILITIES

WHAT THE COMPANY OWES—+ RESERVES + SURPLUS + STOCKHOLDERS INTEREST IN THE COMPANY

ASSETS

WHAT THE COMPANY OWNS— + WHAT IS OWED TO THE COMPANY

FIXED ASSETS

MACHINERY, EQUIPMENT, BUILDINGS, ETC.

EXAMPLES OF FIXED ASSETS

DESKS, TABLES, FILING CABINETS, BUILDINGS, LAND, TIMBERLAND, CARS AND TRUCKS, LOCOMOTIVES AND FREIGHT CARS, SHIPYARDS, OIL LANDS, ORE DEPOSITS, FOUNDRIES

EXAMPLES OF:

PREPAID EXPENSES

PREPAID INSURANCE, PREPAID RENT, PREPAIDD ROYALTIES AND PREPAID INTEREST

DEFERRED CHARGES

AMORTIZATION OF BOND DISCOUNT, ORGANIZATION EXPENSE, MOVING EXPENSES, DEVELOPMENT EXPENSES

ACCOUNTS PAYABLE

BILLS THE COMPANY OWES TO OTHERS

BONDHOLDERS ARE CREDITORS

BOND CERTIFICATES ARE IOU'S ISSUED BY A COMPANY BACKED BY A PLEDGE

BONDHOLDERS ARE OWNERS

A STOCK CERTIFICATE IS EVIDENCE OF THE SHAREHOLDER'S OWNERSHIP

EARNED SURPLUS

INCOME PLOWED BACK INTO THE BUSINESS

NET SALES

GROSS SALES MINUS DISCOUNTS AND RETURNED GOODS

NET INCOME

= TOTAL INCOME MINUS ALL EXPENSES AND INCOME TAXES

www.ingramcontent.com/pod-product-compliance
Lightning Source LLC
Chambersburg PA
CBHW081829300426
44116CB00014B/2520